W9-CJC-825

Finding America's Voice:
A Strategy for Reinvigorating
U.S. Public Diplomacy

Report of an Independent Task Force
Sponsored by the
Council on Foreign Relations

Peter G. Peterson, Chair
Kathy Bloomgarden, Henry Grunwald,
David E. Morey, and Shibley Telhami,
Working Committee Chairs
Jennifer Sieg, Project Director
Sharon Herbstman, Project Coordinator

The Council on Foreign Relations is dedicated to increasing America's understanding of the world and contributing ideas to U.S. foreign policy. The Council accomplishes this mainly by promoting constructive debates, clarifying world issues, producing reports, and publishing *Foreign Affairs*, the leading journal on global issues. The Council is host to the widest possible range of views, but an advocate of none, though its research fellows and Independent Task Forces do take policy positions.

THE COUNCIL TAKES NO INSTITUTIONAL POSITION ON POLICY ISSUES AND HAS NO AFFILIATION WITH THE U.S. GOVERNMENT. ALL STATEMENTS OF FACT AND EXPRESSIONS OF OPINION CONTAINED IN ALL ITS PUBLICATIONS ARE THE SOLE RESPONSIBILITY OF THE AUTHOR OR AUTHORS.

The Council will sponsor an Independent Task Force when (1) an issue of current and critical importance to U.S. foreign policy arises, and (2) it seems that a group diverse in backgrounds and perspectives may, nonetheless, be able to reach a meaningful consensus on a policy through private and nonpartisan deliberations. Typically, a Task Force meets between two and five times over a brief period to ensure the relevance of its work.

Upon reaching a conclusion, a Task Force issues a report, and the Council publishes its text and posts it on the Council website. Task Force reports can take three forms: (1) a strong and meaningful policy consensus, with Task Force members endorsing the general policy thrust and judgments reached by the group, though not necessarily every finding and recommendation; (2) a report stating the various policy positions, each as sharply and fairly as possible; or (3) a "Chair's Report," where Task Force members who agree with the Chair's report may associate themselves with it, while those who disagree may submit dissenting statements. Upon reaching a conclusion, a Task Force may also ask individuals who were not members of the Task Force to associate themselves with the Task Force report to enhance its impact. All Task Force reports "benchmark" their findings against current administration policy in order to make explicit areas of agreement and disagreement. The Task Force is solely responsible for its report. The Council takes no institutional position.

For further information about the Council or this Task Force, please write the Council on Foreign Relations, 58 East 68th Street, New York, NY 10021, or call the Director of Communications at 212-434-9400. Visit our website at www.cfr.org.

Copyright © 2003 by the Council on Foreign Relations®, Inc.

All rights reserved.

Printed in the United States of America.

This report may not be reproduced in whole or in part, in any form (beyond that copying permitted by Sections 107 and 108 of the U.S. Copyright Law and excerpts by reviewers for the public press), without written permission from the publisher. For information, write the Publications Office, Council on Foreign Relations, 58 East 68th Street, New York, NY 10021.

CONTENTS

FOREWORD

When this Independent Task Force first convened in the wake of the September 11, 2001, attacks, it focused on a comparatively contained problem: the growing gulf between the United States and the Arab world and the attendant security risks emanating from a region inflamed. At the time, the country drew strength from the "unconditional support" (in the words of German Chancellor Gerhard Schroeder) and solidarity of allies and friends from all corners of the earth. Much has changed.

In the past year, the Task Force found that negative opinions of the United States and its policies have metastasized. Beyond the threat of a direct attack by al Qaeda and those influenced by that movement, the United States is now facing a more fundamental loss of goodwill and trust from publics around the world. The Task Force argues that this loss has damaged America's ability to protect itself and to attain its foreign policy goals, and that in the run-up to the U.S.-led war in Iraq, botched diplomacy on all sides left a legacy of resentment, fear, and anxiety. Included in this report are polling data showing an Arab world that fears the United States as a threat to its way of life, a Europe that largely does not trust the United States and wants to pull further away, and dwindling support for the U.S.-led war on terror.

The Council's Independent Task Force on Public Diplomacy was formed to devise fresh and creative responses to a problem that has too often received short shrift by the U.S. government. The United States is pelted daily by a range of knee-buckling problems and worse. To deal with them, the United States needs to play all the piano keys, from diplomacy to economic power to military power to public diplomacy. Public diplomacy encompasses how we express our policies to people who might not understand and agree with them, as well as the vehicles we use to reach those people. Without effective public diplomacy, the United States is left with only the soft private words of diplomacy and raw military and economic power.

The Task Force found that in the year since the first version of this report, the administration has taken some promising first steps toward a reinvigorated public diplomacy, but far more is needed to face the urgent and growing problems. Our military victory in Iraq was impressive, but this report asks, "What has the United States gained if it loses the good opinion of mankind?"

This Task Force, chaired by Peter G. Peterson, brought together leading thinkers and practitioners from academia, government, public relations, journalism, and broadcasting. Together this group brought rigorous thought and a much-needed diversity of approaches to this difficult problem. In the following report, the members of the Task Force make a compelling case that hatred and ill will toward the United States and its policies are dangerous and growing, and that radical changes are needed in response.

The Task Force recommends that America must first and foremost bring the concerns of public diplomacy into the heart of the foreign policymaking process. Other recommendations range from specific ideas for greater and better training of our foreign policy professionals to ways to better communicate our messages to ideas for restructuring the foreign policy bureaucracy to manage the overall process more effectively. The Task Force's program is clear and specific and merits the careful attention of policymakers.

My deepest appreciation and admiration go to Task Force chairman Pete Peterson for his thoughtful work and passion for public diplomacy. My thanks also go to Anne Luzzatto and Jennifer Sieg for their tireless help in managing this process and to Sharon Herbstman for her excellent drafting skills. The Council is also grateful to the Ford Foundation and to Harold Pachios and the U.S. Advisory Council on Public Diplomacy for their generous support of the Task Force's work.

Leslie H. Gelb
President
Council on Foreign Relations
June 2003

EXECUTIVE SUMMARY

The United States has a growing problem. Public opinion polls echo what is seen in foreign editorials and headlines, legislative debate, and reports of personal and professional meetings. Anti-Americanism is a regular feature of both mass and elite opinion around the world. A poll by the *Times* of London, taken just before the Iraq war, found respondents split evenly over who posed a greater threat to world peace, U.S. President George W. Bush or then Iraqi leader Saddam Hussein. At the same time, European antiwar protests drew millions, and several national leaders ran successfully on anti-American platforms. Americans at home and abroad face an increased risk of direct attack from individuals and small groups that now wield more destructive power. The amount of discontent in the world bears a direct relationship to the amount of danger Americans face.

What is most surprising is how quickly the tide of sympathy turned. In the immediate aftermath of September 11, 2001, the United States experienced an emotional outpouring of what German Chancellor Gerhard Schroeder called "unconditional solidarity." The cover of the French newspaper *Le Monde* proclaimed "Nous sommes tous Américains," ("We are all Americans"), and in an extraordinary move, NATO members invoked Article V of the common defense treaty, agreeing that an attack against the United States was an attack against all.

Much has changed. What seemed on September 11 to be a problem of America's image in the Muslim world has grown into a larger issue. From Paris to Cairo, from Bonn to Amman, from Madrid and Moscow to Istanbul and Jakarta, ordinary citizens actively oppose fundamental American policy decisions. An independent survey found that in seven of eight nations polled, at least a plurality believed that American foreign policy is having a negative effect on their country.[1] The challenges that have resulted for American diplomacy as leaders respond to popular opinion, from thwarted access to military bases in Turkey to the inability of the United States to gather UN Security Council support for the liberation of Iraq, are serious and the consequences are real.

The president and the administration have taken the first steps to addressing this problem through improving our nation's public diplomacy—that is, the programs and efforts designed to explain and advocate U.S. values and policies directly to foreign publics. While a few encouraging steps have been taken, the administration must do more, and do so urgently. The inability to reach agreement over the war in Iraq has catalyzed simmering resentment and exacerbated political and cultural differences with even our closest allies.

America has a serious image problem. World opinion of the United States has dangerously deteriorated. Around the world, from Western Europe to the Far East, many see the United States as arrogant, hypocritical, self-absorbed, self-indulgent, and contemptuous of others. American culture, language, and industry dominate the world stage in a way that many find discomfiting.

While there is no denying that the United States has substantive differences of policy and position with other states, many of the most controversial U.S. actions might have generated less antagonism with better presentation. From the outright rejection of the Kyoto climate change pact to the seeming dismissal of the International Criminal Court (ICC), the United States appears to be an obstructionist, not a constructive critic. Better by far to have a different approach: one that favors fixing problems where possible and walking away from the negotiating table only as a last option and always with a good explanation for our actions.

Better by far to have a different process: one that would have produced a U.S. proposal to fix Kyoto's flaws (or at the very least list them), rather than making the United States seem callous

---

[1] Pew Research Center for the People and the Press. Poll conducted March 2003, based on surveys of 500 to 1,000 adults in Britain, France, Germany, Italy, Spain, Poland, Russia, and Turkey. The margin of sampling error is between plus or minus 3 and 5 percentage points.

about global warning and dismissive of the 10 years of work by 160 countries that went into the agreement. Washington also could have found a better way to articulate concerns with the ICC, rather than just walking away and signaling a lack of concern.

Rage and deep misunderstanding of America are most marked in the part of the world where aggravated feelings of grievances directed at the United States must be viewed in the context of decline, despair, hopelessness, humiliation, and envy, especially in the face of America's unprecedented—and very visible—affluence and presumed lack of empathy. One of greatest challenges the United States is now facing in the Arab world is the perception that America is both propping up undemocratic regimes and unfairly supporting Israel with indifference to Palestinian suffering and humiliation. Both of these perceptions are constant irritants to the Arab world, and both are examples of where policy and public diplomacy are inextricably intertwined.

Why should the United States care if it is well liked or not? Because at this moment of our greatest strength, we are uniquely vulnerable. Anti-Americanism is endangering our national security and compromising the effectiveness of our diplomacy. Not only is the United States at increased risk of direct attack from those who hate it most, but it is also becoming more difficult for America to realize its long-term aspirations as it loses friends and influence. By standing so powerful and alone, the United States becomes a lightning rod for the world's fears and resentment of modernity, inequality, secularism, and globalization.

The United States faces great challenges abroad: making Iraq a better and safer place, playing a part in Afghanistan, fighting the global scourge of terrorism, and confronting the risk of renewed conflict on the Korean Peninsula. These are not battles that can be won solely with military might, and they cannot be won alone. The United States needs strong and willing partners at every step. To meet these challenges, Washington needs to focus on traditional state-to-state diplomacy, but it must also create a strong and robust public diplomacy—one able to win hearts and minds and show people that the United States can once again be trusted and admired.

The anti-America sentiment seen in the streets is reflected in the actions of foreign leaders. Those who stood with the United States as it liberated Iraq did so in the face of the direct and vociferous opposition of their citizens. What foreign publics think matters to their leaders and therefore must matter to us. As Senator Richard G. Lugar of Indiana, chairman of the Senate Foreign Relations Committee, noted, "The governments of most nations respond to public opinion, whether it is demonstrated in the voting booths or in the streets."[2]

This growing anti-Americanism is a deep and systemic problem that cannot be "managed" with a quick fix, nor with an episodic, defensive, after-the-fact, crisis-driven approach. If not checked, its future consequences will be even more serious.

Taking foreign opinion into account does not mean forsaking U.S. interests, let alone its values. But it is naive not to realize that attitudes abroad can obstruct the success of U.S. policies. So it should be standard operating procedure to consider likely reactions to U.S. moves. Where possible, America should make its policies mesh with those of others. Where this cannot be done, Washington should be unapologetic but at least have a stance it can explain.

The issue here is not allowing the foreign opinion tail to wag the dog of American foreign policy. That would be dangerously wrong. Rather, the United States must take the views and politics and cultural lenses of others into account as it formulates and communicates its policy in order to make that policy both more effective and better understood and accepted.

The lack of serious response to this problem suggests that the United States is falling into two traps. One trap is thinking it does not matter much what others think of America, though all common sense and experience show otherwise. The United States has special responsibilities and must lead and take its lumps in the process. But successful leaders require partners and followers, and those are increasingly in short supply.

---

[2] Opening statement, Senator Richard Lugar, chairman, Senate Foreign Relations Committee, hearing on public diplomacy and Islam, February 27, 2003.

The second danger is that Washington believes it has already taken the necessary steps inside and outside the government to deal with this vast problem. The new steps taken by the president are most welcome, but inadequate. The problem of growing anti-Americanism is enormous, and America's response must be urgent, substantial, and sustained.

This report therefore calls for revolutionary change: from the way Washington shapes and implements U.S. foreign policy objectives to the way it recruits and trains public officials to the way it defines the missions of U.S. embassies and diplomats.

As the most powerful nation in the world, the United States can never be universally loved, and it would be a mistake to try. There are those for whom hatred of the United States is so deep and ingrained and irrational that they are beyond reach. This is a fight for the middle ... and we are losing.

This report is about strategies to address those leaders and people who are touched by anti-Americanism but who remain reachable. The United States can reach these people by listening to their needs and perspectives, by initiating a genuine dialogue, and by taking into account their cultural and political realities as Washington formulates its foreign policies. It is to these ends that this Task Force and its strategy are dedicated.

FINDINGS

The Task Force has made two sets of findings. The first set is about what is going on in the world that has made the need for effective public diplomacy far more urgent.

1. *Anti-Americanism is on the rise throughout the world.* Opinion polling, reporting, editorial comment, legislative debate, and everyday personal contacts tell an alarmingly consistent story—harsh criticism of U.S. positions, culture, and foreign policy have become the norm.

2. *Growing anti-Americanism is increasingly compromising America's safety and constricting our movements.* As the world

becomes more open and democratic, individuals and small groups wield more power to influence global affairs directly, indirectly, and through their governments. This includes extremist groups able to "box above their weight"—to wield power far greater than their numbers, financial wherewithal, or destructive capabilities would suggest. The imperative for effective public diplomacy now requires much wider use of newer channels of communication and more customized, two-way dialogue and debate as opposed to "push-down," one-way mass communication.

The second group of findings is about what is lacking in our government that prevents us from responding more effectively. The administration and Congress have taken first steps. Thus far, however, these initiatives have not made significant headway in meeting the president's own stated objectives. Washington has made a start, but the problem goes far beyond current efforts to deal with it.

3. *Public diplomacy is treated as an afterthought.* The United States has been doing too little about this problem because the country has not absorbed the situation's full urgency and seriousness. Therefore, public diplomacy is all too often relegated to the margins of the policy process, rendering it effectively impotent. Washington must realize that defending the homeland, seeking out and destroying terrorists, and using public diplomacy to make it easier for allies to support the United States and to reduce the lure of terrorism are all parts of the same battle. The concerns of public diplomacy—how U.S. actions and words impact the rest of the world and the outcomes these actions provoke—have not been incorporated into the foundations of the U.S. foreign policy process.

4. *The U.S. government underutilizes the private sector.* Washington is not tapping into the vast talents and resources of the American private sector. While the government lags far behind, the U.S. private sector leads the world in most of the key strategic areas required for effective public diplomacy: technology, film and broadcast, marketing research, and communications.

Public diplomacy will deliver far more bang for the government buck if there is a much-expanded role for the private sector. The Task Force has several reasons for this firm conviction:

- First, target audiences of the U.S. government tend to be foreign governments, and the U.S. government must inevitably observe protocols that can obscure its messages.

- Second, formal U.S. government communications tend to be relatively rigid and involve carefully defined limits.

- Third, the U.S. government may at times require a certain deniability. Private activities can provide that deniability.

- Fourth, it is important to communicate the U.S. belief in democratic and open debate—the give-and-take of a culture that thrives on legitimate criticism and truth. This is a powerful form of public diplomacy.

- Fifth, the U.S. government is unlikely to attract a sufficient number of truly creative professionals to its ranks or to utilize the newest, most cutting edge forms of media, communications, or technology. Furthermore, the Task Force believes media or entertainment "spokespeople" may be more likely to cooperate with private sources, such as nongovernmental organizations (NGOs), than with the U.S. government directly. For example, the Task Force envisions credible and independent messengers from many sectors of American life, including Arab and Muslim Americans—messengers who reflect the complexity and diversity of U.S. society.

5. *U.S. foreign policy is often communicated in a style that breeds frustration and resentment.* U.S. foreign policy is too often communicated in a "push-down" style that does not take into account the perspective of the foreign audience or open the floor for dialogue and debate. Americans are seen as too seldom "listening" to the world while they are defining their interests and defending them abroad. This hit-and-run style breeds frustration and resentment abroad as foreign audiences feel their opinions are being ignored or dismissed.

6. *The United States allocates too few resources to public diplomacy programs.* Public diplomacy programming is severely underfunded both in absolute terms and in comparison to other allocations. For every dollar spent on the military, the U.S. government spends seven cents on diplomacy. And of those seven cents, only one-quarter of one penny is spent on public diplomacy (including exchange and educational programs).

RECOMMENDATIONS

I. Rethink how the United States formulates, strategizes, and communicates its foreign policy.

1. *Make the formulation of foreign policy more sensitive to public diplomacy concerns.* Edward R. Murrow, the legendary newsman whom President John F. Kennedy appointed director of the U.S. Information Agency (USIA), urged that public diplomacy officials be included at "the take offs, not just the crash landings," in other words as foreign policy is made. This would help (1) to ensure that policymakers are aware of the likely reaction of foreign publics to a forthcoming policy; (2) to advise how best to convincingly communicate policies to foreign audiences; and (3) to ensure that U.S. diplomats are prepared to articulate policies before they are announced.

   The Task Force strongly endorses this approach, which inculcates public diplomacy into the ongoing policymaking process and thus makes it "present at the creation." Public diplomacy must be an integral part of foreign policy, not something that comes afterward to sell a foreign policy or to respond to criticism after the fact. It should not decide foreign policy issues, but it must be taken into consideration at the same time as foreign policy is being made. In this way it would help define optimum foreign policies as well as explain how U.S. policies fit the values and interests of other nations, and not just those of Americans. Otherwise, the United States runs into the same problem it did for many years on human rights policy: the president would launch a foreign policy that did not include human rights. Then, when attacked, Washington would roll out the human rights rhetoric, but people abroad would not take it seriously.

2. *Strengthen the public diplomacy coordinating structure.* In the past year, the administration has taken the first steps toward creating an effective Public Diplomacy Coordinating Structure (PDCS), as recommended by this Task Force and others. The newly formed White House Office of Global Communications (OGC) and the Policy Coordinating Committee on Strategic Communications helped to coordinate messages and overall organization during the Iraq war and the ongoing aftermath.

However, strong leadership and increased resources are essential for these structures to accomplish their objectives. This will require an individual leader with regular access to the president, the secretary of state, the secretary of defense, and other top officials. The public diplomacy adviser must have the confidence and trust of the president, as well as a deep strategic and practical understanding of the power of communications in today's global information environment. It must also be this leader's priority to ensure that the new public diplomacy structures will streamline efforts across agencies and departments rather than create even more bureaucratic infighting.

This official's responsibilities should include overseeing the development of strategic public diplomacy priorities, advising the president and senior policymakers on foreign public opinion and communications strategies, and long-range planning of public diplomacy. This individual should also review carefully all presidential statements to consider their impact abroad given what is known about foreign attitudes and sensitivities.

The PDCS should help define communications strategies, streamline public diplomacy structures, and horizontally transfer ownership of these efforts to U.S. government agencies, allies, and private sector partners. The PDCS should resemble the National Security Council in its role as adviser, synthesizer, coordinator, and priority-setter.

The coordinating structure should include members at the assistant-secretary level or above designated by the following: the assistant to the president for national security affairs; the director of the White House Office of Global Communications; the secretary of homeland security; the secretaries of the Departments of State, Defense, Treasury, and Commerce; the attorney general; the directors of central intelligence and the U.S. Agency for International Development (USAID); and the chairs of the Broadcasting Board of Governors (BBG) and the Joint Chiefs of Staff.

3. *Issue a Presidential Decision Directive (PDD) on public diplomacy.* It is essential that the president himself make clear America's commitment to reform its public diplomacy and make it a central element of U.S. foreign policy. The PDD should outline America's new strategy and provide a coordinating structure to harness the government's civilian and military public diplomacy assets.

4. *Initiate a regular evaluation of diplomatic readiness and prioritized spending through a "Quadrennial Public Diplomacy Review" (QPDR).* Modeled on the Quadrennial Defense Review, the public diplomacy review should be conducted by the secretary of state in consultation with the U.S. Advisory Commission on Public Diplomacy.

5. *Improve U.S. capacity to "listen" to foreign publics.* To raise fewer hackles, the United States should listen better. The U.S. government spends only $5 million to $10 million annually on foreign public opinion polling (U.S. businesses spend $6 billion). That amount does not cover the research costs of many U.S. senatorial, gubernatorial, or other political campaigns and is obviously a tiny fraction of U.S. private sector spending in these areas. It is critical that Washington allocate additional research money—both to shape programs and efforts from their inception and to continually monitor, evaluate, and test their effectiveness. The United States should know in advance the likely

reaction and level of resistance to its policies and how America can best communicate them.

6. *Craft messages highlighting cultural overlaps between American values and those of the rest of the world.* To foster a better understanding of U.S. policies, the government should find ways to tie them more closely to U.S. cultural values, including democratic traditions and freedom of expression. The peacekeeping mission in Kosovo or U.S. humanitarian aid to Afghanistan and Iraq should be presented as reflections of American cultural values.

II. Build new institutions to bolster public diplomacy efforts.

1. *Bridge the gap between public and private sector initiatives by creating an independent, not-for-profit "Corporation for Public Diplomacy" (CPD).* The experience of the Corporation for Public Broadcasting is highly relevant, and so the Task Force proposes a similar entity as a focal point for private sector involvement in public diplomacy.

   The CPD would have the capacity to:

   - Act as a "heat shield" between the government and controversial projects;

   - Act as a focal point for private sector involvement in public policy;

   - Accept private sector grants;

   - Attract media and personalities not willing to work directly with the U.S. government;

   - Provide more credible messengers for skeptical audiences; and

   - Support regional voices of moderation and independent media.

2. *Establish an "Independent Public Diplomacy Training Institute" (IPDI).* This new entity, independent of the government, would draw on the best talent and techniques from U.S.

corporations and universities to help recruit and prepare a new breed of Foreign Service professionals to perform the critical roles of public diplomacy.

3. *Establish a Public Diplomacy Reserve Corps.* This agency, patterned on the Federal Emergency Management Agency's disaster-relief model, would augment U.S. and overseas operations; mandate an action plan, a skills database, periodic training, updated security clearances, simplified reentry regulations, and modification of temporary appointment requirements; and recruit prestigious private sector experts from relevant professions for short-term assignments.

III. Improve the practice of public diplomacy.

1. *Through State Department reforms, ensure that public diplomacy is central to the work of all U.S. ambassadors and other diplomats.* Diplomats engage in the basic tasks of public diplomacy at embassies all over the world, and many do an admirable job. On the whole, however, U.S. diplomats must be far better prepared.

   In an age when heads of state converse directly—and when headquarters' instructions and field reporting occur in real time—the role of the ambassador as a public diplomat becomes increasingly important. Public advocacy and local language skills are essential for today's ambassadors. To the extent that they are not taking on these tasks, ambassadors must be comfortable with and seek out opportunities to meet with editorial boards, as well as make public statements and appear on television and in other indigenous media. Delegated authority to speak for the United States without excessive clearance requirements and increased understanding by policymakers of the need to provide timely content are critical to their success.

2. *Further enhance training for U.S. ambassadors.* Currently, the State Department offers a two-week training seminar for new ambassadors, and only a small amount of that time is devoted

to public diplomacy. The State Department usually provides a one-to-two-page printed summary on public diplomacy in the country to which the ambassador is assigned. Two days are devoted to media skills training. However, this is not mandatory, and not all ambassadors participate.

The training seminar should be expanded along the lines of the State Department's new program for career officers. For public affairs officers, the State Department has proposed a newly enhanced training plan scheduled to take effect in September 2003 that increases training to as long as nineteen weeks.

3. *Expand the range of America's messengers abroad.* The United States should find locals to shoulder some of the burden by identifying and developing credible local messengers such as young and moderate Arabs and Muslims, mullahs, journalists, and talk-show personalities who can criticize flaws within their own regions more credibly than a U.S. diplomat ever could.

The United States should also make much more use of credible and independent messengers to highlight the diversity of American life, including the Arab-American firefighters and police officers who rushed to the World Trade Center scene; Arab and Muslim Americans, including women and children, who died or lost loved ones on September 11; and Muslim Americans who are thriving in the United States and can attest to the respect their religion receives, including sports stars like Muhammad Ali, other celebrities, and leaders from such fields as business, science, and medicine.

4. *Foster increasingly meaningful relationships between the U.S. government and foreign journalists.* Too often, foreign reporters feel they are treated as second-class citizens relegated to the fringe of U.S. outreach efforts. To the extent that the U.S. government marginalizes foreign journalists, it alienates a group of highly effective, highly credible messengers. Washington must therefore continue to increase foreign press access to high-level American officials, insisting that senior policymakers take time to brief foreign journalists at U.S. foreign press centers and make

themselves available for one-on-one interviews. This coordinated and consistent effort to engage foreign journalists more effectively must take place at all times—not just during crises.

5. *Support voices of moderation in other countries, with particular attention over the longer term to the young, in order to empower them to engage in effective debate through means available or created in their societies.* The United States should not have to make its case alone. America must encourage the debate and dialogue within Islam about the hijacking of its spiritual soul by supporting—often through third parties such as nongovernmental organizations—regional voices of moderation and peace and an open and free press.

6. *Adopt an "engagement" approach that involves listening, dialogue, debate, and relationship building.* Historically, U.S. public policy has been communicated largely via the "push-down" method, which lacks both a broad reach and an adequate explanation to foreign media. Policy is created, speeches given, press releases written, and press conferences held—all with a primary focus on addressing the U.S. media. In this "push-down" approach, the government too often does not engage in open discussion of how it arrived at its policy decisions. Communications geared primarily toward a domestic U.S. audience assume a keen understanding of the U.S. system of government—knowledge that foreign publics often lack. Washington frequently fails to link its policies to the values of others, or even explicitly to our own values, and thus misses the opportunity to show how these policies are a reflection of U.S. freedom and democracy.

7. *Respond to satellite broadcasting and Internet-age realities.* Current trends in information technology are transforming how the world communicates and learns. The impact of satellite broadcasting was made obvious to all during the Iraq war. Diplomats, members of the Broadcasting Board of Governors, and others in public diplomacy will also need to understand that the

Internet revolution is fundamentally changing the relationship between information content and communications channels, though in most developing countries the Internet is still far from broadly integrated. The Broadcasting Board of Governors, with its disproportionate emphasis on radio and television broadcasting, should give higher priority to new digital technologies, including content-rich, language-specific Internet services.

Though at present the Internet is of somewhat limited value in reaching the majority of America's target audiences abroad, the online audience it does reach is influential and should not be ignored. This is especially true in countries with state-controlled media, where the Internet (which is more difficult to censor) can be the only source of free information. As the simple one-to-many broadcasting model of the past gives way to a more complex array of push-and-pull interactions between content providers and audiences, public diplomacy must utilize all the available communications resources.

8. *Create bridges between U.S. society and others using common cultural pursuits in every genre of art, music, theater, religion, and academia.* In the short term, public diplomacy is a tool to influence opinions and mobilize foreign publics in ways that support immediate interests and policies. In the long term, the United States needs programs to build an open dialogue with key foreign publics, as well as personal and institutional relationships founded on shared ideas and values, such as student and professional exchanges, art exhibits, American libraries abroad, and academic endowments. To be effective, America's long-term and short-term efforts should be linked in a comprehensive strategy. Some of these programs may be administered through embassies (art exhibits, American libraries), others through NGOs (health services) and academic institutions.

IV. Improve funding and allocation.

1. *Bring public diplomacy funding in line with its role as a vital component of foreign policy and national security.* America has few higher priorities today than public diplomacy. In order to develop an effective and comprehensive program, public diplomacy must be funded at significantly higher levels. The marginalization of public diplomacy has created a legacy of underfunded and uncoordinated efforts. A budget is needed far in excess of the approximately $1 billion currently spent by the State Department and the Broadcasting Board of Governors in their public diplomacy programming.

2. *Build congressional support for public diplomacy.* Congress' role in authorizing and appropriating resources for public diplomacy is crucial, and increased resources are far more likely if Congress has a sense of ownership over public diplomacy and an appreciation of public diplomacy's linkages to foreign policy. Close cooperation with key members of Congress must be a priority for senior participants in the Public Diplomacy Coordinating Structure.

CONCLUSION

In sum, the United States has significantly underperformed in its efforts to capture the hearts and minds of foreign publics. The marginalization of public diplomacy has left a legacy of underfunded and uncoordinated efforts. Lack of political will and the absence of an overall strategy have rendered past public diplomacy programs virtually impotent in today's increasingly crowded communications world. While sound public diplomacy is not a silver bullet for America's image problem, making it a serious component of the foreign policymaking process is a vital step toward ensuring the nation's security.

TASK FORCE REPORT

BACKGROUND

The Nature of the Problem

The United States has a growing problem. Public opinion polls echo what is seen in foreign editorials and headlines, legislative debate, and reports of personal and professional meetings. Anti-Americanism is a regular feature of both mass and elite opinion around the world. A poll by the *Times* of London, taken just before the war in Iraq, found respondents split evenly over who posed a greater threat to world peace, U.S. President George W. Bush or then Iraqi leader Saddam Hussein. At the same time, European antiwar protests drew millions, and several national leaders ran successfully on anti-American platforms. Americans at home and abroad face an increased risk of direct attack from individuals and from small groups that now wield more destructive power. The amount of discontent in the world bears a direct relationship to the amount of danger Americans face.

What is most surprising is how quickly the tide of sympathy turned. In the immediate aftermath of September 11, 2001, the United States experienced an emotional outpouring of what German Chancellor Gerhard Schroeder called "unconditional solidarity." The cover of the French daily *Le Monde* proclaimed "Nous sommes tous Américains," ("We are all Americans"), and in an extraordinary move, NATO members invoked Article V of the common defense treaty, agreeing that an attack against the United States was an attack against all.

The United States is an unprecedented military and economic force; its culture, language, and industry dominate the world stage. Why should the United States care if it is well liked or not? Because at this moment of our greatest strength, the United States is uniquely vulnerable. Anti-Americanism is endangering

U.S. national security and compromising the effectiveness of our diplomacy. Not only is the United States at increased risk of direct attacks from those who hate it most, but it is also becoming more difficult for us to realize our long-term aspirations as we lose friends and influence.

The few national leaders who stood with Washington as the United States invaded Iraq did so in the face of the direct and vociferous opposition of their citizens. What their publics think matters to them and therefore must matter to us. As Senator Richard G. Lugar of Indiana, chairman of the Senate Foreign Relations Committee, noted, "The governments of most nations respond to public opinion, whether it is demonstrated in the voting booths or in the streets."[3]

Growing anti-Americanism is a serious problem. It is deep and systemic and cannot be "managed" with a quick fix, nor with an episodic, defensive, crisis-driven approach. Down the line, the United States will have greater costs if it does not see this as a profound, growing sentiment about America, about how Americans think, and about how the United States relates to the world. Where the reasons for anti-Americanism are unjustified, the United States must combat the sentiment; where they ring true, Washington must take them into account as it shapes U.S. policy moving forward.

The lack of serious response to this problem suggests that the United States is falling into two traps. One trap is thinking it does not matter much what others think of America, though all common sense and experience show otherwise. The United States has special responsibilities and must lead and take its lumps in the process. But successful leaders require partners and followers, and those are increasingly in short supply. Everything the United States undertakes in the world is becoming that much harder without the active support of those who would help.

The second danger is that the administration believes it has already taken steps inside and outside the government to deal with this vast problem and that the problem is on its way to being fixed. The

---

[3] Opening statement, Senator Richard Lugar, chairman, Senate Foreign Relations Committee, hearing on public diplomacy and Islam, February 27, 2003.

new steps taken by the president are welcome but mostly inadequate. The problem of growing anti-Americanism is enormous, and America's response must be urgent, substantial, and sustained.

The challenges the United States now faces cannot be addressed by force alone. The world is littered with examples of military force's failing to stanch sustained terrorist uprisings. In Spain, Israel, Ireland, and the former Soviet republics, innocent people have died and democracy has suffered without any increase in security. We cannot capture every terrorist nor destroy every weapon. Rather, we must learn to confront the hatred, desperation, and frustration that are the breeding ground where terrorism thrives.

Nor can this battle be won by spin alone. Empty promises and rhetoric hurt America's cause as it loses credibility and trust from those the United States is trying to reach. This is especially true in the echo chamber that is today's media environment, where misleading statements and inconsistencies are highlighted, critiqued, and broadcast repeatedly to every corner of the earth.

Finally, this battle cannot be won alone. We need strong and willing partners and allies throughout the world to help break up financing rings, to share in policing and intelligence work, to patrol borders, and to provide development and reconstruction aid, manpower, and expertise. The United States also needs allies to stand with it, help explain the U.S. way of life to the world, and absorb some of the negative sentiment.

Taking foreign opinion into account does not mean forsaking U.S. interests, let alone our values. But it is naive not to realize that attitudes abroad can obstruct the success of American policies. So it should be standard operating procedure to consider others' likely reactions to U.S. moves. Where possible, America should make its policies mesh with those of others. When this cannot be done, Washington should be unapologetic but at least have a stance it can explain.

Rebuilding America's image will be a monumental and long-term task. The United States is facing great challenges now. While the U.S. private sector has led the world in the communications revolution, the government lags far behind. The United States is politically and culturally at odds with much of the world, including some of its closest allies. Competing noise from a proliferation of messages and messengers makes it increasingly difficult for our voice to break through. Cynical audiences are not receptive to what America has to say. And Washington has stripped bare the institutions that spread U.S. values and goodwill during the Cold War.

Further, the United States must build this capacity in a new foreign policy environment. Globalization, the increased speed and greatly diminished cost of processing and transmitting information, growing Internet penetration, the reach of 24/7 television programming, global news media, satellite television, mobile phones, populist movements fueled by religious and sectarian beliefs, and wider public participation in international affairs are central characteristics of the 21st-century foreign policy environment. As a result, the fundamental role of public information and its relationship to foreign policy have changed.

The Task Force commends the efforts this administration has taken so far to listen and to tell the U.S. story to the world: the formation of an Office of Global Communications (OGC), the appointment of an undersecretary of state for public diplomacy, and the executive order creating a Policy Coordinating Committee (PCC) on Strategic Communications to help coordinate interagency public diplomacy efforts are all important steps. But these steps alone have not done enough to counter the onslaught of anti-Americanism. This report therefore also calls for revolutionary change: from the way Washington shapes and implements its foreign policy objectives to the way the United States recruits and trains public officials to the way America defines the missions of its embassies and diplomats.

Why Anti-Americanism Matters

Growing anti-Americanism increases the threat of direct attack. Terrorist attacks against America's homeland and interests abroad make clear that U.S. national security can no longer rest on favorable geography, military strength, and economic power alone.

The world has become a more democratic place in the last decade, a change driven largely by new communications technologies and advances in travel and weaponry. Small groups of nonstate actors now wield unprecedented power both to influence governments and to act on their own. This applies to nongovernmental organizations (NGOs), corporations, and all types of interest groups. It also applies to independent terrorists with destructive designs who now, for the first time, possess the capability to wreak mass destruction. These small, volatile groups of individuals—what *New York Times* columnist Thomas Friedman has called "the superempowered angry man"—cannot be contained by the rules of traditional statecraft.

The al Qaeda phenomenon is a potent illustration: a group of like-minded, geographically dispersed individuals are now able to find each other, share information instantly and anonymously, move money, organize actions, obtain weapons, and spread their message to the world.

The amount of discontent in the world bears a direct relation to the amount of danger America faces. As hatred of the United States grows, so does the pool of potential terrorists. In parts of the world, a new generation is growing up learning to hate the United States.

Unfriendly foreign publics will make it more difficult to prevent future attacks. The United States will never convince the fanatics who hate us most, and it would be a waste of resources to try. In the Muslim world today, America's most pressing battle is for the political and social middle. And we are losing.

Opinion polling from the Islamic world shows some shocking results: more than 70 percent polled do not believe that Arabs carried out the September 11 attacks.[4] Many believe that the United States is at war with Islam and invaded Iraq solely to control that nation's oil fields or to support some nefarious plot with Israel. Those who hate the United States are more likely to offer support and shelter to terrorists and provide future recruits.

---

[4] See Gallup/*USA Today*, "Poll Results," February 27, 2002, and Andrea Stone, "Many in Islamic World Doubt Arabs Behind 9/11," *USA Today*, February 27, 2002.

The United States needs partners in its struggle against terrorism, yet it is losing them. Even in friendly countries, anti-Americanism is creating pressure on foreign leaders not to cooperate with the United States on security measures. As populations around the world have more access to information and communications technologies, they have more ability not only to act on their own, but also to put pressure on government leaders as well.

The United States needs determined and strong partners throughout the world to work on policing, border patrol, disrupting terrorist financial networks, and reconstruction and development efforts that are crucial to U.S. military actions. If the United States keeps losing influence with European, Asian, and moderate Middle Eastern countries, it cannot win the battle to make America safer—no matter how great its military power.

The United States is just beginning to see the effects of this groundswell in Europe, South Asia, and elsewhere where governments must balance domestic political pressures with support for the United States. U.S. military action in Iraq has catalyzed the sentiment that had been growing since September 11. Antiwar and anti-U.S. protesters numbered in the millions, and even America's most sympathetic allies have little political room to maneuver.

Standing alone makes America more vulnerable. If Washington accepts that anti-American sentiment correlates with the amount of violence directed at the United States, then it becomes evident that America needs allies to stand shoulder to shoulder with the United States to help it absorb some of the ire from the rest of the world. Right now, as the sole remaining superpower, the United States stands out as a lightning rod, attracting hate and blame for all the ills of globalization, the fears of military might, and the resentment of Western affluence.

Anti-Americanism is depleting America's much-needed "soft power." The loss of "soft power"—the power to persuade, attract, and lead by example—will undercut U.S. foreign policy and military efforts.[5] Like the Cold War, U.S. efforts in Afghanistan

---

[5] See Joseph S. Nye, Jr., *The Paradox of American Power: Why the World's Only Superpower Can't Go It Alone* (New York: Oxford University Press, 2002).

and Iraq promise to be long, protracted, and in large part about winning hearts and minds to U.S. political values—democracy, transparency, and the rule of law. During the Cold War, U.S. administrations spoke directly to leaders and to people behind the Iron Curtain about the dangers of their political systems and showed them a different, more attractive way of life. Without this credibility, America runs the risk of becoming nothing more than an occupying military force.

The inability or unwillingness of other governments to ally themselves with the United States is leading to a constriction of movement on the world stage and a loss of U.S. ability to shape the world. History suggests that the United States will not be the sole dominant world force forever. This moment is America's opportunity to help shape the world as it goes through a time of great unrest and transition. The influence the United States has now, in supporting new democracies, security, and stability, can bring a more peaceful and prosperous world. The United States must therefore do everything possible to defuse growing anti-Americanism and regain the understanding and respect of the world.

The Roots of Anti-Americanism

When looking for underlying reasons for this rash of anti-Americanism, the United States is faced with a complex etiology of policy decisions, misperceptions, poor communication on its part, willful manipulation of its actions and image by others, and structural causes related to America's dominant position on the world stage. Further, all of the above are exacerbated by political pressures—both at home and abroad—and by a backlash against the U.S. use and threat of force (no matter how justified).

Structural Factors. As the sole superpower, the richest nation on earth, and a nation flexing its muscle, the United States will never be universally loved. Much of the anti-American sentiment emanating from poor countries grows from the fertile soil of vast inequity. The United States is strong; others are weak. American global leadership is evident; other states have uncertain roles. Much of this resentment stems from problems that are long term and intractable—such as global poverty—and that cannot be fully addressed in the near term but that catalyze deep envy and anger and demand a visible response nonetheless.

Rage and deep misunderstanding of America are most marked in the parts of the world where aggravated feelings of grievances directed at the United States must be viewed in the context of decline, despair, hopelessness, and even humiliation, especially in the face of America's unprecedented—and very visible—affluence. In the Arab world, for example, this tension has been an incalculable factor in inflaming passions. It allows the reality and the image of the United States to become a potent and easily manipulated symbol of all that is wrong at home and in the world. By standing so powerful and alone, the United States becomes a lightning rod for the world's fears and resentment of modernity, inequality, secularism, and globalization.

Cultural Factors. There is a growing cultural gulf between the United States and much of the world. These two groups view the world through vastly different cultural lenses that impose conflicting sets of values. Not just in the Middle East, but increasingly in Europe as well. While others view the United States as arrogant and unilateralist, America fumes at the unwillingness of others to accept responsibility. In both instances, domestic political pressures largely drive these stances. For example, the political right in the United States wields substantial power right now. But many of the social values they stand for are anathema to many Europeans. Washington's official support for the death penalty is seen as barbaric; the American culture of guns and the reemergence of churchgoing ways conflict with a Europe that is becoming more secular and shifting in cultural values toward the left. There are also strong cultural divides between Europeans and Americans on attitudes toward military buildup and the use of force.[6]

Another source of tension is the broad sweep of American culture. Hollywood movies, television, advertising, business practices, and fast-food chains from the United States are provoking a backlash from some who feel that their local culture is being overrun.

---

[6]"Living with a Superpower," *The Economist*, January 4, 2003.

And there are powerful religion-based clashes with the more devout Islamic world. Practitioners of extreme forms of Islam see America's largely secular state and influence as heretical. As the United States is the propagator and symbol of this very visible culture spreading throughout the world, Americans are seen as the enemies of God.

Resentment of U.S. Policy. U.S. foreign policy decisions are based on assessments of national interests; thus Washington cannot just change policies to suit foreign public opinion. But the United States has to realize that consequences in public opinion are part of the picture and must take these attitudes into account when presenting U.S. policies in the first place.

Many of the charges of hypocrisy have to do with U.S. support for autocratic and corrupt governments while it espouses the primacy of American democratic values, U.S. perceived unbalanced support for Israel, a perceived lack of empathy for the hardship of the Palestinians in the West Bank, and the suspicion of U.S. motives in Iraq and the rest of the region.

There are powerful trade-offs in Washington's backing authoritarian governments, and the administration should take a much harder look at the costs of these policies. In the Middle East, the United States needs to do a far better job of conveying a national commitment to justice and progress for both Arabs and Israelis, even as Washington supports the state of Israel.

U.S. Rhetoric. Actions speak louder than words; nonetheless, words and style still matter a great deal in U.S. dealings with the rest of the world. Many of the most provocative American policies might have gene-rated less antagonism with better presentation. From the outright rejection of the Kyoto climate change pact to the seeming dismissal of the International Criminal Court (ICC), the United States appears to be obstructionist, not a constructive critic.

Better by far to have a different approach: one that would have produced a U.S. proposal to fix Kyoto's flaws (or at the very least list them), rather than making the United States seem callous about global warning and dismissive of the ten years of work by 160 countries that went into the agreement. Washington also could have found a better way to articulate concerns about the ICC, rather than just walking away and signaling a lack of concern.

Some of the anti-American sentiment is certainly exacerbated, if not caused, by the bellicose and dismissive rhetoric that has come from Washington. Utterances from Washington carry great weight around the world, and remarks such as President Bush's use of the term "crusade" for our fight against terrorism and his reference to the "axis of evil," as well as Secretary of Defense Donald Rumsfeld's dismissal of France and Germany as "old Europe," do much to antagonize those abroad.

Intentionally Incited Hatred. Another problem the United States is facing is the intentional anti-American vitriol that is sometimes spewed by state-controlled news media in the Muslim world. Washington often confronts "friendly" government-supported media, such as in Saudi Arabia and Egypt, that despite being major recipients of U.S. assistance, tolerate and even encourage media bashing of the United States.

How to Respond

The problems now facing the United States cannot be solved with force or with empty spin. America needs to mobilize another dimension in U.S. foreign policy—one that has been underemphasized in recent decades. This will require a fundamental shift in the way U.S. officials make and implement foreign policy and the ways in which they conduct themselves abroad and at home—in short, a renewed commitment to the concerns and tools of public diplomacy.

Above all else, the United States needs a system of public diplomacy that is able to reach key decision-makers and ordinary citizens abroad more effectively. It is no longer enough to speak only though official diplomatic channels; America must be able to speak directly to foreign publics. The United States needs to improve its ability to convey broad messages regarding overall American values, as well as real-time, focused messages and rapid-fire crisis responses using traditional and new channels of communication. At the same time, the United States needs to create better conduits for information to flow back to policymakers, so that the U.S. knows how its messages and actions are being received and can adjust and prepare accordingly.

As with the Cold War, the United States is facing a long and protracted challenge over a way of life. More than ever, America needs the influence, the attractiveness, and the moral standing to show the world not just that it is strong, but that America is not the enemy. The United States must demonstrate that it represents a way of life marked by democracy, openness, and the rule of law—and that this is a life worth aspiring to.

This administration has taken a few positive first steps but has offered little in the way of results. Polling numbers reinforce what is already seen, that the amount and vitriol of anti-Americanism is growing throughout the world and that the United States has not effectively spread messages in support of its foreign policy objectives.

For all the great challenges the United States is now facing, the administration has had some promising success. The Broadcasting Board of Governors (BBG) has made a popular success of Radio Sawa, the Arabic-language radio station broadcasting popular music and news throughout the Middle East. The BBG more recently launched Radio Farda with Persian-language broadcasts into Iran in December 2002. The Voice of America (VOA) has launched an Arabic-language website and is increasing programming in Cantonese and Indonesian.

Other efforts have met with less success. Short documentary-style commercials about Muslim life in the United States cost $15 million and found little airtime in their target countries. And two times in the past year, the Pentagon has floated ill-received plans of its own to influence foreign publics. While these plans may have struck the wrong chord, they bring to light the frustration and urgency felt from America's lack of effective public diplomacy.

FINDINGS

The Task Force has made two sets of findings. The first set is about what is going on in the world that has made the need for effective public diplomacy far more urgent.

1. *Anti-Americanism is on the rise throughout the world.* Opinion polling, reporting, editorial comment, legislative debate, and everyday personal contacts tell an alarmingly consistent story—harsh criticism of U.S. positions, culture, and foreign policy have become the norm.

2. *Growing anti-Americanism is increasingly compromising America's safety and constricting its movements.* As the world becomes more open and democratic, individuals and small groups wield more power to influence global affairs directly, indirectly, and through their governments. This includes extremist groups able to "box above their weight"—to wield power far greater than their numbers, financial wherewithal, or destructive capabilities would suggest. The imperative for effective public diplomacy now requires much wider use of these channels of communication and more customized, two-way dialogue and debate as opposed to "push-down," one-way mass communication.

   The second group of findings is about what is lacking in our government that prevents us from responding more effectively. The administration and Congress have taken first steps. Thus far, however, these initiatives have not made significant headway in meeting the president's own stated objectives. Washington has made a start, but the problem goes far beyond current efforts to deal with it.

3. *Public diplomacy is treated as an afterthought.* The United States has been doing too little about this problem because the country has not absorbed the situation's full urgency and seriousness. Therefore, public diplomacy is all too often relegated to the margins of the policy process, rendering it effectively impotent. Washington must realize that defending the homeland, seeking out and destroying terrorists, and using public diplomacy to make

it easier for allies to support the United States and to reduce the lure of terrorism are all parts of the same battle. The concerns of public diplomacy—how U.S. actions and words impact the rest of the world and the outcomes these actions provoke—have not been incorporated into the foundations of the U.S. foreign policy process.

4. *The U.S. government underutilizes the private sector.* Washington is not tapping into the vast talents and resources of the American private sector. While the government lags far behind, the U.S. private sector leads the world in most of the key strategic areas required for effective public diplomacy: technology, film and broadcast, marketing research, and communications. This Task Force believes that public diplomacy will deliver far more bang for the government buck if there is a much-expanded role for the private sector. We have several reasons for this firm conviction:

- First, target audiences of the U.S. government tend to be foreign officials, and the government must inevitably observe diplomatic protocols in communicating with these counterparts.

- Second, formal U.S. government communications tend to be relatively rigid and involve carefully defined limits.

- Third, the U.S. government may at times require a certain deniability that private citizens can provide.

- Fourth, it is important to communicate American belief in democratic and open debate—the give-and-take of a culture that thrives on legitimate critiques and, at its best, admits weaknesses and uses truth as the most powerful form of public diplomacy.

- Fifth, the U.S. government is unlikely to attract a sufficient number of truly creative professionals within the government or to utilize the newest forms of media communications or technology. Furthermore, we believe media or entertainment "spokespeople" may be more likely to cooperate with private sources, such as NGOs, than directly funded government programs.

5. *U.S. foreign policy is often communicated in a style that breeds frustration and resentment.* U.S. foreign policy is too often communicated in a "push-down" style that does not take into account the perspective of the foreign audience or open the floor for dialogue and debate. Americans are seen as too seldom "listening" to the world while they are defining their interests and defending them abroad. This hit-and-run style breeds frustration and resentment abroad as foreign audiences feel their opinions are being ignored or dismissed.

6. *The United States allocates too few resources to public diplomacy programs.* Public diplomacy programming is severely underfunded both in absolute terms and in comparison to other allocations. For every dollar spent on the military, the U.S. government spends seven cents on diplomacy. And of those seven cents, only one-quarter of one penny is spent on public diplomacy (including exchange and educational programs).

RECOMMENDATIONS

I. Rethink how the United States formulates, strategizes, and communicates its foreign policy.

1. *Make the formulation of foreign policy more sensitive to public diplomacy concerns.* Edward R. Murrow, the legendary newsman whom President John F. Kennedy appointed director of the U.S. Information Agency (USIA), observed after the Bay of Pigs fiasco in Cuba that public diplomacy officials should be in on "the take offs, not just the crash landings." Unfortunately, the current structure tends to create those crash landings. It has produced a series of examples that even some of America's best friends abroad find baffling. From the outright rejection of the Kyoto climate change pact to the seeming dis-

missal of the International Criminal Court, the United States appears to its allies as obstructionist, rather than a constructive critic. This does not mean that America should change its policies to suit others' wishes. That is unrealistic. But it does mean that Washington must be aware of the cost of anti-Americanism and form and communicate U.S. foreign policy with a public diplomacy dimension.

Murrow urged that public diplomacy officials be included when foreign policies are made for several reasons: (1) to ensure that policymakers are aware of the likely reaction of foreign publics to a forthcoming policy; (2) to advise how best to convincingly communicate policies to foreign audiences; and (3) to ensure that U.S. diplomats are prepared to articulate policies before they are announced.

The Task Force strongly endorses this approach, which inculcates public diplomacy into the ongoing policymaking process and thus makes it "present at the creation." Public diplomacy must be an integral part of foreign policy, not something that comes afterward to sell the foreign policy or to respond to criticism after the fact. It should not decide foreign policy issues, but it must be taken into consideration at the same time as foreign policy is being made. In this way it would help define optimum foreign policies as well as explain how U.S. policies fit the values and interests of other nations, and not just those of Americans. Otherwise, the United States runs into the same problem it did for many years on human rights policy: the president would launch a foreign policy that did not include human rights. Then, when attacked, Washington would roll out the human rights rhetoric, but people abroad would not take it seriously.

2. *Strengthen the public diplomacy coordinating structure.* In the past year, the administration has taken the first steps toward creating an effective Public Diplomacy Coordinating Structure (PDCS), as recommended by this Task Force and others.

During the Iraq war, both the Office of Global Communications (OGC), formally established by the White House in March 2003, and the Policy Coordinating Committee on

Strategic Communications, established in September 2002 and co-chaired by the acting undersecretary of state for public diplomacy and public affairs and the special assistant to the president for democracy, human rights, and international operations, took first steps in terms of messaging and interagency coordination. The OGC conducts a daily call with representatives from interested agencies and departments including the Department of Defense, the National Security Council, and the Department of the Treasury. The OGC also publishes and widely distributes a daily briefing with talking points and messages of the day.

However, strong leadership and increased resources are essential for these structures to accomplish their objectives. Strong leadership requires an individual with regular access to the president, the secretary of state, the secretary of defense, and other top officials. The public diplomacy adviser must have the confidence and trust of the president, as well as a deep strategic and practical understanding of the power of communications in today's global information environment. It must also be this leader's priority to ensure that new public diplomacy structures will streamline efforts across agencies and departments rather than create even more bureaucratic infighting.

This official's responsibilities should include overseeing the development of strategic public diplomacy priorities, advising the president and senior policymakers on foreign public opinion and communications strategies, and long-range planning of public diplomacy. This individual should also review carefully all presidential statements to consider their impact abroad given what is known about foreign attitudes and sensitivities.

A dedicated secretariat is also essential to carrying out the work of the PDCS. The secretariat should consist of a small, full-time staff drawing on expertise in civilian and military agencies that carry out public diplomacy, corporate communications and marketing, and NGOs interested in communicating U.S. interests and values abroad. The secretariat should report directly to the PDCS and should not be viewed as the satellite staff of any one department. Members of the secretariat should be detailed by their agencies on a non-reimbursable basis. U.S. agencies not included in the secretariat should provide advisory and operational support as issues and circumstances warrant. The secretariat should be led by an officer selected from the Senior Foreign Service or the Senior Executive Service or be a military officer of flag rank or a professional of comparable level recruited from the private sector. It is important that the secretariat's director and staff be sensitive to different civilian and military organizational cultures and to department perceptions—and misperceptions—of the PDCS and its mandate.

The PDCS and a dedicated secretariat must have an adequate budget and the authority to coordinate timely communications strategies and information dissemination by civilian and military agencies. The PDCS must be able to command, among other things: (1) expanded analyses of foreign public opinion and structures of influence through government departments and contracts with independent research organizations; (2) the development of credible themes and messages for crisis response and long-term communications strategies tailored to different audiences in different cultures; (3) the identification of appropriate media outlets and other information-dissemination channels; (4) the production and commercial acquisition of information products; (5) recruitment and "best practices" training; (6) the deployment of qualified individuals to countries and regions with critical needs; and (7) surge broadcasting for crisis communications.

The PDCS should help define communications strategies, streamline public diplomacy structures, and horizontally transfer ownership of these efforts to U.S. government agencies, allies, and private sector partners. The PDCS should resemble the National Security Council in its role as adviser, synthesizer, coordinator, and priority-setter.

The coordinating structure should include members at the assistant-secretary level or above designated by the following: the assistant to the president for national security affairs; the director of the White House Office of Global Communications; the secretary of homeland security; the secretaries of the

Departments of State, Defense, Treasury, and Commerce; the attorney general; the directors of central intelligence and the U.S. Agency for International Development (USAID); and the chairs of the Broadcasting Board of Governors and the Joint Chiefs of Staff.

3. *Issue a Presidential Decision Directive (PDD) on public diplomacy.* It is essential that the president himself make clear America's commitment to reform its public diplomacy and make it a central element of U.S. foreign policy.

Early in 2001, the Bush administration undertook a review of previous efforts to integrate public diplomacy into the policy process that was intended to provide guidance before the new administration would implement its own interagency coordinating structure. This review is still not complete.

Many in the administration may feel they have made public diplomacy a genuine priority. Certainly some new and useful steps have been taken. In June 2003, Congress authorized a new advisory group to investigate and report on public diplomacy efforts in the Arab and Muslim world. However, to people who follow these matters—here and abroad—public diplomacy does not yet look like a genuine priority of the U.S. administration at all. It is essential that President Bush himself make clear the U.S. government's commitment to reforming public diplomacy and making it a central element of U.S. foreign policy.

Core elements of the presidential directive should include: (1) a clear policy and strategy to strengthen the U.S. government's ability to communicate with foreign publics; (2) a strong coordinating structure for the U.S. government's civilian and military public diplomacy assets; (3) a requirement that all regional and functional National Security Council Policy Coordinating Committees assess the potential implications for foreign public opinion of policy options under consideration and develop communications strategies—which are indispensable—in concert with policy implementation; (4) guidance on public diplomacy resources, training, programs, budgets, and technology; (5) special attention to relations with NGOs, international organizations, commercial media outlets, and coalition allies; and (6) a schedule of tasks and benchmarks to evaluate progress in achieving reforms.

4. *Initiate a structured evaluation of diplomatic readiness and prioritized spending through a "Quadrennial Public Diplomacy Review (QPDR)."* This evaluation, similar to the existing Quadrennial Defense Review, should be conducted by the secretary of state in consultation with the U.S. Advisory Commission on Public Diplomacy. It should replace budget-driven reviews of the status quo with strategy-based assessments of themes; the current state of affairs; and diplomatic readiness, requirements, and capabilities, thereby providing a much-needed, long-term national information strategy.

5. *Improve our capacity to "listen" to foreign publics.* To raise fewer hackles, the United States should listen better. The first step toward less antagonistic policies and improved communications is a deeper and more nuanced understanding of foreign cultures, attitudes, and likely reactions to U.S. policies. This can be accomplished by a variety of means, including public opinion polling, information gathering by trained and linguistically competent embassy staff, and the garnering of information from the private sector and friendly governments.

The U.S. government spends only $5 million to $10 million annually on foreign public opinion polling (U.S. businesses spend $6 billion). The amount the U.S. government spends does not cover the research costs of many U.S. senatorial, gubernatorial, or other political campaigns and is obviously a tiny fraction of U.S. private sector spending in these areas. It is critical that Washington allocate additional research money—both to shape programs and efforts from their inception and to continually monitor, evaluate, and test their effectiveness. The administration should know in advance the likely reaction and level of resistance to its policies and means of communication.

6. *Craft messages highlighting cultural overlaps between American values and those of the rest of the world.* In the short term, public diplomacy seeks to influence opinions and mobilize publics in ways that support specific U.S. interests and policies. The short-term focus is primarily, but not exclusively, on issues. By contrast, in the long term, public diplomacy promotes dialogue in ways that are politically, culturally, and socially relevant. Ideally, the two should be linked in a comprehensive public diplomacy strategy. Creating this strategy involves finding sufficient common ground to permit dialogue.

To attract and strengthen the hands of people who are in a potential frame of mind to help the United States, America needs to make them part of what it does in ways that reflect their interests and values. If recent polls are correct, the Muslim world responds much more favorably to U.S. values and freedoms than they do to U.S. policies. Washington must leverage the common goods of freedom and democracy to build consensus and ownership.

By repeating lies about America's economic, social, and cultural values, America's enemies in the war on terrorism have been able to rally a tremendous amount of support. As former U.S. ambassador to the United Nations Richard Holbrooke once asked, "How can a man in a cave out-communicate the world's leading communications society?" The United States needs to be able to counter these vitriolic lies with the truth and with culturally resonant messages of its own.

Recent opinion studies report that while many U.S. policies are deplored, there is a mystique surrounding America's culture, values, and economy. Thus, to foster a better understanding of U.S. policies, Washington should find ways to tie them more closely to American cultural values, including the nation's democratic traditions and extraordinary capacity for self-criticism and self-correction. Values that should be highlighted include strength of family, religious faith, expansive social safety nets, volunteerism, freedom of expression, the universal reach of education and its practical consequences in economic prosperity, and America's achievements in science and medicine.

As a means of building interest and confidence in American news sources, U.S. communications should include honest and sympathetic news coverage and advice on important local and regional problems that might be of practical help in the areas of health care, agriculture, and daily life. These messages should be imbued with both empathy and understanding. And, where possible, Washington should present U.S. foreign policies as a reflection of American cultural values, e.g., during the peace-keeping mission in Kosovo or during U.S. humanitarian aid efforts to Afghanistan and Iraq.

II. Build new institutions to bolster public diplomacy efforts.

1. *Bridge the gap between public and private sector initiatives by creating an independent, not-for-profit "Corporation for Public Diplomacy" (CPD).* The Task Force believes the experience of the Corporation for Public Broadcasting (CPB) is highly relevant, and we propose a similar entity as a focal point for private sector involvement in public diplomacy.

   The CPB is not part of a cabinet-level department and is therefore somewhat independent of direct political influence. This structure permits the CPB, as a corporation with tax-exempt status under Section 501(c)(3) of the U.S. tax code, to receive private sector grants, which have been substantial. (Media magnate Walter Annenberg gave the CPB hundreds of millions of dollars, for example, to administer a school-based initiative.) The CPB has a seven-member board of directors appointed by the president of the United States. Four directors come from the president's party, and the other three must be of the opposing party.

   The CPB has been deeply involved in the establishment or support of such programs as *Sesame Street, The News Hour with Jim Lehrer*, Bill Moyers' documentaries, and American Playhouse. Many of the most widely acclaimed public television programs would likely not have arisen or flourished had they been the sole prerogative of the U.S. government.

The CPB makes grants to a variety of individual producers and stations that in a sense have to defend what they are doing. The CPB and inferentially the government, which provides about $350 million of public money, are not seen as directly responsible for the programming on CPB-supported stations.

In an analogous structure, an organization such as a Corporation for Public Diplomacy would likewise seek to leverage private sector creativity and flexibility. It could receive private sector grants and would attract media and personalities potentially less willing to work directly with U.S. government agencies. Its proposed structure also takes advantage of the fact that private media often communicate American family values, religious commitments, and the merits of democracy more effectively than do government officials. Groups such as the Advertising Council and the ad hoc group of Hollywood executives, producers, engineers, and creative talents who joined together after September 11 (which has done enormous work for other public causes) should be enlisted to help the CPD.

In projecting America's messages, Washington must be especially mindful of something that every good salesman understands—if you do not trust the messenger, you do not trust the message. The Task Force strongly believes that the United States can avoid this problem by using private sector partnerships and new approaches such as a new CPD. As with any public-private partnership, there will be tension between the two worlds. In this case, it is important to remain mindful of the potential contradiction between the freedom of the private sector and the need for consistency of message and image. The public-private messengers will be especially effective coming from Muslim and Arab Americans who seek to build bridges and improve cross-cultural relations but who might sometimes be reluctant to work for the U.S. government or who may be dismissed by foreign audiences if they are seen to do so.

Finally, the Task Force believes the CPD would be well positioned to support independent indigenous new media channels (e.g., satellite, radio, and TV networks or private satellite TV stations with joint venture programming with existing Arab stations) or joint think tanks on issues with countries in the region.

2. *Establish an "Independent Public Diplomacy Training Institute" (IPDI).* The long-term need to attract and train modern Foreign Service professionals is analogous to the need for those who understand the ever-increasing role of economics in foreign policy—"geo-economics"—in contrast to the earlier dominance of strategic Cold War thinking. This new independent entity could help in recruiting and preparing a new breed of foreign professionals who understand the critical role of public diplomacy. The IPDI would also attract the best talent and techniques from U.S. corporations and universities involved in research, marketing, campaign management, and other relevant fields. The IPDI would then apply private sector "best practices" in communications and public diplomacy and become an important training ground for the next generation of public diplomacy and governmental officials.

The IPDI would offer training and services in public opinion research, cultural and attitudinal analysis, segmentation, database management, strategic formulation, political campaign management, marketing and branding, technology and tactics, communications and organizational planning, program evaluations, and studies on media trends. In coordination with, and as a supplement to, the State Department's National Foreign Affairs Training Center, such an institute would enhance the quality of public diplomacy programs and the skills of future foreign affairs professionals.

3. *Establish a Public Diplomacy Reserve Corps.* This agency, patterned on the Federal Emergency Management Agency's disaster-relief model, would augment U.S. and overseas operations; mandate an action plan, a skills database, periodic training, updated security clearances, simplified reentry regulations, and modification of temporary appointment requirements; and recruit prestigious private sector experts from relevant professions for short-term assignments.

III. Improve the practice of public diplomacy.

1. *Through State Department reforms, ensure that public diplomacy is central to the work of all U.S. ambassadors and other diplomats.*[7] Our diplomats—not all of whom share Secretary of State Colin Powell's media skills—should be far better prepared. In an age when heads of state converse directly—and when headquarters' instructions and field reporting occur in real time—the role of the ambassador as a public diplomat becomes increasingly important. Public advocacy and local language skills are essential for today's ambassadors. Ambassadors must be comfortable with and seek out opportunities to meet with editorial boards, make public statements, and appear on television and other indigenous media. Critical to their success are delegated authority to speak for the United States without excessive clearance requirements and an increased understanding by policymakers of the need to provide timely content.

   The budget and operational authority of the undersecretary of state for public diplomacy and public affairs must be increased substantially. We also believe public diplomacy should be made the full-time job or at least a primary responsibility of a deputy assistant secretary in each of the State Department's regional bureaus.

2. *Further enhance training for U.S. ambassadors.*[8] Currently, the State Department offers a two-week training seminar for new ambassadors, and only a small amount of that time is devoted to public diplomacy. This is not nearly enough. The State Department usually provides a one-to-two-page printed summary on public diplomacy in the country to which the ambassador is assigned. Two days are devoted to media skills training. However, this is not mandatory, and not all ambassadors participate. The Task Force strongly advocates a much-increased

---

[7]See Appendix A for further details of suggested State Department organizational reforms.

[8]See Appendix B for a detailed Mission Program Plan for public diplomacy that will require, among other things, each ambassador to establish a mission Public Diplomacy Task Force.

training seminar along the lines of the new program designed for career officers.

Since the first version of this report, the State Department has designed and approved a new training scheme for career public affairs officers scheduled to take effect in September 2003. As proposed, this plan will increase the amount of training officers receive from two weeks to as long as nineteen weeks with separate concentrations for information officers and cultural affairs officers. The majority of training will be done by career officers, with outside professionals brought in for one week of media training.

3. *Expand the range of America's messengers abroad.* The United States must more fully employ credible messengers who complement official government sources. To encourage genuine dialogue and avoid an "us vs. them" approach, it is essential that the administration identify and develop indigenous talent (e.g., mullahs, talk show personalities, scientists, health-care providers, business leaders, as well as Arab and other Muslim students who were recruited as part of the existing State Department program for foreign students of all nationalities, studied at American universities and colleges, and have returned to their home countries), as well as other independent messengers who can criticize extremism with more credibility than spokespersons from Washington. In thus fostering the free flow of ideas, the administration should be fully aware that these messengers will sometimes be critical of the United States. By the same token, however, these dialogues should not in any way shrink from countering vigorously the various conspiracy theories and lies that are disseminated about the United States and, of course, about themselves.

The Task Force also envisions attracting credible television properties and personalities such as MTV and *Sesame Street* to play a substantial role. Likewise, the printed press remains highly influential in these foreign countries.

Unfortunately, many foreign sources are often more readily believed than U.S. sources, and the United States should therefore make ample use of such commentaries. Indeed, Washington should cooperate and coordinate with its allies in a variety of areas in the U.S. public diplomacy effort. Allies such as the United Kingdom have announced their renewed commitment to external communications, and these efforts should be coordinated at the highest possible levels in both multilateral and bilateral talks whenever possible.

4. *Foster increasingly meaningful relationships between the U.S. government and foreign journalists.* Too often, foreign reporters feel they are treated as second-class citizens relegated to the fringe of U.S. outreach efforts. To the extent that the U.S. government marginalizes foreign journalists, it alienates a group of highly effective, highly credible messengers. Washington must therefore continue to increase foreign press access to high-level American officials, insisting that senior policymakers take time to brief foreign journalists at U.S. foreign press centers and make themselves available for one-on-one interviews. This coordinated and consistent effort to engage foreign journalists more effectively must take place at all times—not just in crises.

The new Office of Global Communications has already taken some positive steps in this direction, such as inviting representatives of foreign media to watch the most recent State of the Union address with Deputy Defense Secretary Paul Wolfowitz. The administration can go even further by establishing a summit that brings together members of the foreign press and high-level government officials to discuss foreign policy. This meeting could be held in an informal setting and bring in foreign journalists located in Washington and New York as well as journalists from abroad. It would provide these reporters with rare access to high-level U.S. officials, including even the president, and show that the U.S. government is committed to fostering a dialogue with both foreign and domestic journalists on important issues. These meetings would illustrate the basic point that the "listen and engage" approach applies to senior officials, not simply to our public diplomacy professionals.

5. *Support voices of moderation, with particular attention over the longer term to the young, in order to empower them to engage in effective debate through means available or created in their societies.* The young make up an unprecedented and increasing portion of the huge population bulge in the Middle East and other areas of great frustration with the United States. Despair at high unemployment and a lack of future prospects, combined with fundamentalist, anti-Western education, makes the young likely recruits for a terror campaign.

Radical Islam's assault on America and the West is also an assault on moderate and secular Islam in the vast majority of the Muslim world. Moderate voices are often not heard above the din of the fanatics. The United States must therefore encourage debate within Islam about the radicals' attempts to hijack Islam's spiritual soul. The United States should support participatory communications, dialogue, and debate among these groups through, for example, the use of radio and television talk shows and new interactive media forums. A good example is Secretary of State Colin Powell's 90-minute MTV dialogue with young people in Brazil, India, Russia, Italy, Egypt, and the United Kingdom in February 2002 that reached 380 million households worldwide.

The United States should also significantly increase support for moderate independent media in the Middle East and Central Asia. Washington followed this policy successfully during the Cold War in the former Soviet Union and Eastern Europe and more recently in the Balkans. USAID helped support a nascent pluralistic television environment in Russia. Today more than 2,000 nongovernmental local television broadcasters are operating in the former Soviet Union.

6. *Adopt an "engagement" approach that involves listening, dialogue, debate, and relationship building.* Historically, U.S. public policy has been communicated largely via the "push-down" method, which lacks both a broad reach and an adequate explanation to foreign media. Policy is created, speeches given, press releases written, and press conferences held—all with a

primary focus on addressing the U.S. media. Many U.S. messages are delivered by a limited number of official messengers, with a primary foreign audience of foreign governments and international organizations, not foreign publics. In this "pushdown" approach, the government too often does not engage in much open discussion of how it arrived at its policy decisions. Communications geared toward a domestic U.S. audience assume a keen understanding of the U.S. system of government—knowledge that foreign publics often lack. Washington frequently fails to link U.S. policies to the values of others, or even explicitly to our own values, and thus misses the opportunity to show how they are a reflection of American freedom and democracy.

7. *Respond to satellite broadcasting and Internet-age realities.* Current trends in information technology are transforming how the world communicates and learns. Diplomats need to understand that the Internet will, over time, fundamentally change the relationship between information content and communications channels, though it is still far from broadly integrated in most developing countries. Therefore, the Internet is currently of somewhat limited value in reaching most of our target audiences. At the same time, however, the audience it currently reaches is an influential one and should certainly not be ignored. As the simple one-to-many broadcasting model of the past gives way to a more complex array of push-and-pull interactions between content providers and audiences, public diplomacy must utilize all the available communications resources.

Since American public diplomacy has limited resources and is unable to reach 100 percent of any given population, it must utilize modern technologies to identify, prioritize, and target those who must be reached. High-priority communications targets might include attitudinal segments that are supportive or potentially supportive of the West and need further information and encouragement, or they might include the large population of younger people in many Arab and Muslim countries. Products in one medium, such as a satellite TV interview, can be used in other media formats such as print, websites, radio, and videocassettes.[9]

The international broadcasting arm of the U.S. government includes the entities of the Broadcasting Board of Governors: Voice of America, Radio Free Europe/Radio Liberty, Radio and TV Marti, Radio Free Asia, and Worldnet Television. Together they reach about 100 million people weekly in 65 languages.

A few key developments deserve emphasis, particularly those that illustrate the interactive, "two-way" dialogue approach emphasized in this report. Prominent among these is the Middle East Radio Network (MERN) created in the spring of 2002. Known in Arabic as "Radio Sawa," this station aims to attract young Arab adults. Delivered via local FM and AM radio and digital satellite, the station is still in the audience-building phase, so most of its programming is Middle Eastern and American music, with newscasts twice an hour. Its plans include gradually adding components, and eventually there will be audience voting for favorite songs, recorded questions from listeners about America and U.S. foreign policy, call-in discussions, and pieces on young people, women's issues, and health. In other words, MERN will interact with its audience and the underlying message will be respect for each other and each other's opinions. MERN is also building an Arabic-language website that announcers will constantly promote on the air. On that website will be key U.S. documents, including the only Arabic-language text in cyberspace of the U.S. Constitution. This approach may become a model for all the languages of U.S. international broadcasting.

---

[9]The State Department's International Information Programs website, usinfo.state.gov. continues to leverage the power of the Internet in addressing important international issues. During the Iraq war, the State Department put up an Iraqi Update Site, the Iraqi Human Rights Report, and a link to Radio Free Iraq accessible from anywhere in the world. See Barry Fulton, *Leveraging Technology in the Service of Diplomacy: Innovation in the Department of State,* PricewaterhouseCoopers Endowment for the Business of Government, E-Government Series, March 2002, pp. 24–25, www.pwcglobal.com.

8. *Create bridges between American society and others using common cultural pursuits in every genre of art, music, theater, religion, and academia.* In the short term, public diplomacy is a tool to influence opinions and mobilize foreign publics in ways that support immediate interests and policies. In the long term, the United States needs programs to build an open dialogue with key foreign publics, as well as personal and institutional relationships founded on shared ideas and values, such as student and professional exchanges, art exhibits, American libraries abroad, and academic endowments. To be effective, U.S. long-term and short-term efforts should be linked in a comprehensive strategy. Some of these programs may be administered through embassies (art exhibits, American libraries), others through NGOs (health services) and academic institutions.

Ever since the Cold War ended, Washington has been stripping bare the institutions designed to share U.S. culture and values. Overseas projects such as English-language libraries have been dismantled, and the number of scholarships for foreign students to study at U.S. institutions has dropped from 20,000 a year in the 1980s to 900 today.

The results of these programs are hard to measure directly, but it can be inferred from experience that they are a valuable mechanism for spreading respect for U.S. values, increasing an understanding of democratic institutions, and enhancing the attractiveness of the United States.

IV. Improve funding and allocation.

1. *Bring public diplomacy funding in line with its role as a vital component of foreign policy and national security.* The marginalization of public diplomacy has created a legacy of underfunded and uncoordinated efforts. For example, the approximately $1 billion spent annually on the Department of State's public diplomacy programs and U.S. international broadcasting is one twenty-fifth of the nation's international affairs budget.

From 1993 to 2001, overall funding for the State Department's educational and cultural exchange programs fell more than 33 percent from $349 million to $232 million (adjusted for inflation). Over the past decade, exchanges in societies with significant Muslim populations declined—even as populations in these countries were increasing. State Department exchanges with Indonesia, the Philippines, Malaysia, and Thailand decreased 28 percent; and in Egypt, Saudi Arabia, and Yemen exchanges fell 21 percent. Moreover, in Pakistan, Afghanistan, Bangladesh, and India the decline was 34 percent. Thus, as the population in countries with significant Muslim populations increased by an estimated 16 percent per capita, State Department per capita spending in these countries decreased by more than one-third. Similar decreases in funding can be seen in the budget for international broadcasting, and Voice of America listening rates in the Middle East have in the recent past averaged only about two percent of the population. Finally, there have been drastic cutbacks in many U.S. information libraries and "America Houses."

To make public diplomacy the kind of priority the administration has talked about would involve a budget far in excess of the approximately $1 billion currently spent by the State Department and the Broadcasting Board of Governors in their public diplomacy programming. As a point of reference, just one percent of the Defense Department's proposed budget of $379 billion would be $3 billion to $4 billion. This pales in comparison to the $222 billion American companies invest annually on overseas advertising. The marginal increases in funding now being considered on Capitol Hill will have insufficient impact and will not be commensurate with the problems this report describes nor with the reforms for which it calls.

The bottom line: U.S. public diplomacy must be funded at significantly higher levels—with money phased in over several years, tied to specific objectives, and monitored closely for effectiveness, including the possible use of test campaigns.

2. *Build congressional support for public diplomacy.* This must be done through sustained oversight and the formation of a new congressional committee structure, probably within the relevant committees, such as the Senate Foreign Relations and House

International Relations Committees. Congress' role in authorizing and appropriating resources for public diplomacy is crucial, and increased resources are far more likely if Congress has a sense of ownership over public diplomacy and an appreciation of public diplomacy's linkages to foreign policy. To this end, the Senate Foreign Relations Committee has expressed sustained interest in the work of this Task Force.

CONCLUSION

In sum, the United States has significantly underperformed in its efforts to capture the hearts and minds of foreign publics. The marginalization of public diplomacy has left a legacy of underfunded and uncoordinated efforts. Lack of political will and the absence of an overall strategy have rendered past public diplomacy programs virtually impotent in today's increasingly crowded communications world. While sound public diplomacy is not a silver bullet for America's image problem, making it a serious component of the foreign policymaking process is a vital step toward ensuring the nation's security.

ADDITIONAL AND DISSENTING VIEWS

I endorse the policy thrust of this report. However, I do so with several reservations relating to its failure to mention some issues that are central to public diplomacy and to a successful war on terrorism. For example, the report correctly highlights "U.S. support for autocratic and corrupt governments" as a source for Arab frustration as well as "high unemployment and a lack of future prospects." But it fails to highlight equally the anger with U.S. policies toward Israel and the pains of the Israeli occupation of Palestinian territories. In that, the report dismisses a major source of frustration and anger and misses the point—the need to understand the causes in order to contemplate remedies.

When addressing U.S.-bashing in some Arab media, the report ignores Arab- and Muslim-bashing in some American media, which are equally irresponsible. In that, the report appears righteous when it comes to "us" and condescending when it is "them," a notion that perpetuates resisting self-criticism at a time this is required of all of us, not only of the others.

Raghida Dergham

We endorse the broad thrust of the report with the following additional point. The report's recommendations to create a Corporation for Public Diplomacy and an Independent Public Diplomacy Training Institute should be more explicit in identifying the roles and comparative advantages of government and the private sector. We support the intent of recommendations that seek to benefit from the skills, flexibility, and creative imagination of the private sector. Strong partnerships with nongovernmental organizations, especially in international exchanges and public opinion research, have long been central to effective public diplomacy. For all their strengths, however, private organizations represent particular interests. Strategies and investments in public diplomacy must reflect the public interest as determined by the Congress, executive branch departments, and the American people.

Barry Fulton
Bruce Gregory
Walter Roberts

While I support most of the Task Force's prescriptions, I do not believe that the solution to our "image" problem consists in our developing ways to tie our policies more closely to our cultural values. The problem is much deeper.

The distinction between our culture and our policies is quite dubious. Our policies are a reflection of our culture. This distinction between who we are and how we behave strikes me as, in large part, a pollster's creation. The statement "I really like Saddam Hussein and Osama bin Laden, I just disagree with their policies" makes no sense. Ask someone who says he likes us but not our policies which policies he is referring to. Is he against the aid we provide Egypt, protecting Kuwait from Iraq in 1991, trying to solve the Israeli-Palestinian conflict, or siding with Muslims against Christians in numerous conflicts around the world? "Our policies" is too general a term to be informative. Unfortunately, emphasizing this distinction between liking us and deploring our policies is often nothing more than a disguised way of saying, "Put pressure on Israel to eliminate a grievance and you will win our hearts and minds."

Perhaps most important, the problem of hearts and minds transcends the policy domain. Unfortunately, the Arab world is laboring under a grievance, and it is very real. However, the core of this grievance is not our policies, but the lack of political legitimacy of the region's regimes. This has at least three consequences. First, since these regional leaders oversee domestic failures, they try to deflect attention away from these failures and attach them to someone else. As the dean of Middle East historians, Bernard Lewis, put it, anti-Israeli and anti-American criticisms are very often "the only grievances that can fully and safely be expressed in Arab countries."

Second, Arab leaders privately admit that their lack of political legitimacy results in a hesitancy to provide a public imprimatur for peace compromises, since these leaders do not like getting out ahead of their publics. This lack of leadership might be the single most tragic reason for the lack of peace culture in the Middle East, the lack of progress in the Arab-Israel peace process, and the fact that there has been no delegitimation of suicide bombing as a tool or substitute for negotiations.

Third, the lack of legitimacy has meant the United States has incurred the wrath of Arab publics at large amid a sense that the United States, as a backer of autocratic regimes, is indifferent to their plight, whereupon they conclude that we are only interested in their oil and not in their "human rights."

While we must do all we can to improve our image through public diplomacy, enhancing the democratic legitimacy of Arab governments—not simply tying our policies more closely to our culture—is the key to a successful relationship with the Arab world. President Bush's actions in Iraq and his policy of pushing for greater democracy and women's rights in the Arab world are good first steps toward ensuring a successful public diplomacy program. Let's stay the course.

Martin Gross

The most stunning reaction to our Iraq enterprise did not come, as so many had predicted, from the Arab street, but from the European street. In hindsight it is not really surprising that the highly emotional and in many ways untypical response to September 11 did not endure. As far as Western Europe is concerned, the underlying cause for this is persuasively analyzed in *Of Paradise and Power,* in which Robert Kagan argues that, for understandable reasons, Western Europeans are trying to eschew force. This rather utopian notion works in Western Europe but does not necessarily apply elsewhere, even within other parts of Europe. Secretary of Defense Donald Rumsfeld's remark about old-new Europe, while perhaps impolite, is absolutely accurate. The lessons are that the United States must make a huge effort in supposedly friendly countries that we have neglected and that anti-Americanism may not be quite as sweeping or undifferentiated as gross poll numbers would suggest. It is also possible to exaggerate the effect of such phrases as the "axis of evil."

Henry Grunwald

I agree with many of the report's recommendations but would give highest priority to an expanded role for the private sector, namely the establishment of a Corporation for Public Diplomacy.

Bette Bao Lord

I see no reason for a Corporation for Public Diplomacy. It would be divisive and not relevant in the brief period when policies have to be formulated and expressed. It would take away from the sense of urgency we should have now.

I do not think the report captures an appropriate sense of urgency and the need for immediate action to be taken.

Presidents and White House staffs are extremely knowledgeable about public opinion, polling, and focus groups, as well as about the importance of formulating policies to appeal to voters. What is necessary is that that knowledge and expertise, plus the expertise of private citizens, be used in foreign policy matters. Everyone knows how important domestic public opinion is to every administration. We are now learning that foreign public opinion can be important, even crucial, to the success of our foreign policy.

Lewis Manilow

Having the BBG sit as a member of a Public Diplomacy Coordinating Structure that would include the director of central intelligence, the secretary of defense, and the secretary of state, as recommended by the Task Force, would have a chilling effect on the notion of the independence and journalistic integrity of U.S. international broadcasting.

Broadcasting is already moving in innovative directions to address the war on terrorism, and it needs the independence and flexibility of its current structure to continue this progress. The BBG's implementation of both MERN and Radio Free Afghanistan has resulted in unprecedented cooperation between VOA and our surrogate broadcasters. The integration of VOA and RFE/RL broadcasts on a single frequency in Afghanistan makes the most of the VOA and surrogate missions: providing local news and information about the countries to which we broadcast, providing U.S. and international news, and presenting the policies of the United States. If the BBG were placed under the purview of a new coordinating structure, suggesting that our message was centrally controlled, it is likely that our surrogate corporate broadcasters would resist such cooperative ventures.

If the U.S. government sees fit to create such an oversight structure, the BBG might benefit from its insights, research, and guidance. But the BBG should not be a member. Congress set the journalistic standards for the BBG and gave it a structure at arm's length from the foreign policy establishment to protect those standards. But it also provided that the secretary of state's membership and participation on the board would provide the mechanism necessary to give the BBG the widest range of foreign policy guidance. The current structure of the board—acting as a firewall to protect broadcast journalism from political and other pressures and providing deniability to the secretary of state about our broadcasts—is appropriate and beneficial. Preserving this firewall and deniability—not as a fiction, but a reality—could be undermined by BBG membership in this new body.

I must also take issue with the Task Force's recommendation of a full-time chief executive officer (CEO) of the BBG (Appendix C). In addition to its chairman, the board already has a president-appointed International Broadcasting Bureau (IBB) director, who also serves as the BBG chief of staff. But more important, the Broadcasting Board of Governors serves as a collective CEO, having since its inception made decisions by consensus in a bipartisan manner.

Each governor serves on numerous committees—VOA, RFE/RL, RFA, OCB, Middle East, China, and Russia. In this way, president-appointed and Senate-confirmed BBG governors, four Democrats and four Republicans of high caliber, become experts in the various regions where we broadcast to over 100 million people in over 60 languages. Governors serve as committee chairs with real authority to present initiatives to the full board, thus multiplying and maximizing the effectiveness of the BBG. The introduction of a full-time CEO is unnecessary and would not have a positive effect.

The BBG's record of achievement since its independence four years ago shows that the current structure is not broken. In fact, it is working very well. The seeds of MERN preceded the intense national debate on countering terrorism by nearly a year. In early 2001, the Broadcasting Board issued a white paper on creating an Arab-language network that would speak to the large populations of young Arabs on the transmission networks that they listen to and that we control. Our research in the area made it clear that there was a media war going on in the region, and the United States did not have a horse in that race. Now we do. And we agree with the Task Force that we need to build similar networks that both appeal to foreign audiences and accomplish our foreign policy mission.

A new initiative to marry our broadcast mission to the market by using the most sophisticated and modern broadcasting techniques in order to present our programming to substantially larger audiences has also been initiated by this board. The foundation of MERN was built on research and, to use the Task Force's own words, we are using research "both to shape programs and efforts from their inception and to continually monitor, evaluate, and test their effectiveness." We face a complex political and media environment in which to deliver our message, and we must take our markets into account when developing our programming in order to gain the largest listenership. The Task Force notes that our challenge is not just to adjust public diplomacy, but also to revolutionize it. At the BBG, we have already begun this process.

The BBG's mission is unique, as is our organizational structure. That structure facilitates the mission. Our programs are not easily classified with the public diplomacy programs of other federal agencies. While we have a foreign policy mandate, we pursue it through journalism. This both serves our national security interests and buys us credibility with our audience. As the Task Force report itself states, "If you do not trust the messenger, you do not trust the message."

Norman J. Pattiz

The proposals to involve the private sector are misleading. First, using "credible and independent messengers" is not a new idea; USIA has employed the technique for decades. For example, USAID has sent many "American Participants" (Amparts) abroad. Second, simply attracting "truly creative professionals" and using "the newest, most cutting edge forms of media, communications, or technology" is not enough. The professionals must have a thorough understanding of the foreign target audiences, and the media and technology must be suited to the audience.

The report seems oblivious to some of the basic public diplomacy activities that U.S. diplomats at embassies all over the world engage in on a regular basis. Ambassadors, DCMs (Deputy Chiefs of Mission), and PAOs (Public Affairs Officers) engage in conversations all the time with editors, writers, and other nongovernmental opinion leaders, in which they explicate U.S. policy and explain American society, culture, and values. The report seriously exaggerates the extent to which they are constrained in doing so. Likewise, on the question of foreign "media bashing," these same U.S. officials do not hesitate to raise such complaints when appropriate.

William A. Rugh

While I support the endorsement of innovative programming such as MERN—or in the more current context, METN—a note of caution is in order. It is my understanding that the initiation of MERN was accompanied by the elimination of VOA Arabic radio broadcasts. I believe this is a mistake. The Task Force's endorsement of MERN should not be interpreted as support for the elimination of core VOA language broadcasts—whether on radio or on television. The over-30 year-old elements in Arab society should not be abandoned. The Voice of America and its hard-earned record of credibility represent 60 years of investment by the United States and are assets that should not be discarded readily. Nor would I regard MERN necessarily as a desirable prototype for broadcasts in other languages in other areas, as the report suggests. The broadcast formula should be tailored to the conditions of a particular region and audience and not to a predetermined American domestic commercial model established for other purposes. In any event, VOA core programs should be carefully preserved in order to maintain a more substantive presentation for influential audience targets. If particular current VOA programs are weak, improve them. If facilities are inadequate, strengthen them. But do not discard established VOA broadcasts willy-nilly in favor of short-term tactical operations designed for particular situations.

I do not believe the Task Force report as a whole gives sufficient attention to the impact of the U.S. military, and certainly of the Pentagon, in forming foreign public opinion about American policies and actions. This is particularly true in such developments as Afghanistan and Iraq. The U.S. military is present in one way or another in over 60 countries. What the Pentagon says or what local commanders and units do has an enormous impact on the reaction of foreign publics, and hence foreign governments, to the United States. Coordination and cohesion in the public comments (as well as actions) of the U.S. military must be observed and maintained through the mechanisms suggested in this report at both the highest levels of the Defense Department and the level of the local commanders in-country. Divisions in the public projection of U.S. actions and views simply provide elements hostile to the

United States with considerable opportunities for exploitation and, at the least, lead to confusion as to U.S. policy and motives.

While I certainly agree that more attention should be paid by the executive branch to foreign journalists both in the United States and abroad, I believe it is also necessary to note that communications with media cannot be compartmentalized. American media—the television news networks, the wire services, and some major newspapers—all have extensive operations abroad, and much of what the world learns about the United States comes from the information provided through these channels. So in communicating with American media, the audience is not solely domestic. There are no walls at the borders blocking transmission of information. The U.S. government's communication with American media must take into account that foreign publics are involved as well.

The report properly points to the sharp reductions in the exchange programs with countries that have significant Muslim populations and recommends a substantial increase in present levels. I would give this recommendation much greater emphasis and broader application than the report does. The exchange program in all its variations is critical for the long-term impact on attitudes toward this country and merits substantial increases across the board even as the United States focuses on more immediate needs. In this regard, the problems of provision of timely visas in the current security-conscious atmosphere must be resolved so that prospective students and desirable visitors, even critics, are not discouraged from entering the United States.

Barry Zorthian

TASK FORCE MEMBERS

PETER ACKERMAN is the Managing Director of Crown Capital Group Incorporated, a private investment firm. He is the co-author of *Strategic Nonviolent Conflict*, published in 1994, and *A Force More Powerful: A Century of Nonviolent Conflict*.

ROGER AMES is the Chairman and Chief Executive Officer of Warner Music Group (WMG). Before joining WMG, Mr. Ames was President of the PolyGram Music Group, at the time the world's largest and most profitable music company.

DONALD BAER is the Senior Executive Vice President, Strategy and Development, at Discovery Communications, Inc. He served as Assistant to the President and White House Director of Strategic Planning and Communications under President Bill Clinton and was an Assistant Managing Editor of *U.S. News & World Report*.

ALI BANUAZIZI is Professor of Cultural Psychology at Boston College, where he is also the Co-Director of the Program in Middle Eastern and Islamic Studies.

KATHY BLOOMGARDEN is the Chief Executive Officer of Ruder Finn, Inc., one of the world's largest independent public relations agencies.

JOAN GANZ COONEY is the co-founder and Chairman of the Executive Committee of Sesame Workshop.

GEOFFREY COWAN is Dean of the Annenberg School for Communication at the University of Southern California. Cowan has

---

Note: Task Force members participate in their individual and not institutional capacity.

*The individual has endorsed the report and submitted an additional or a dissenting view.

served as Director of the Voice of America, Director of the International Broadcasting Bureau, and Associate Director of the U.S. Information Agency (USIA).

RAGHIDA DERGHAM* is the Senior Diplomatic Correspondent for the London-based *Al-Hayat,* the leading independent Arabic daily newspaper. She writes a regular weekly strategic column on international political affairs and is one of the few female political commentators on American, Arab, and worldwide TV networks.

JOSEPH DUFFEY served as Director of the U.S. Information Agency from 1993 to 1999. He was Assistant Secretary of State for Education and Cultural Affairs under President Jimmy Carter.

LYNN FORESTER DE ROTHSCHILD is the President and Chief Executive Officer of ELR Holdings LLC, an international private investment company. A former member of the National Information Infrastructure Advisory Council and the Secretary of Energy Advisory Council and a U.S. representative on various international trade and technology missions, she also serves on several charitable and corporate boards.

BARRY FULTON* is Director of the Public Diplomacy Institute at George Washington University and a Research Professor in the School of Media and Public Affairs. He concluded his career in USIA as Associate Director for Information. During 30 years as a Foreign Service Officer, he served in Brussels, Rome, Tokyo, Karachi, and Islamabad.

PETER GEORGESCU is Chairman Emeritus of Young & Rubicam, Inc., a network of preeminent commercial communications companies dedicated to helping clients build their businesses through the power of brands. He served as the company's Chairman and Chief Executive Officer from 1994 until January 2000. Mr. Georgescu is a member of the Media and Advertising Hall of Fame.

MARC CHARLES GINSBERG served as the U.S. Ambassador to Morocco from 1994 to 1998. Following his return to the United States, he served as U.S. Special Envoy for Mediterranean Security and Trade Policy. He is also President of Layalina Productions, Inc., a new U.S. not-for-profit Arab-language television production company that is developing a new generation of information and entertainment programs for Middle East media outlets.

BRUCE GREGORY* is the Executive Director of the Public Diplomacy Council and serves on the board of the Public Diplomacy Institute at George Washington University. He served on the faculty at the National War College from 1998 to 2001 and was Executive Director of the U.S. Advisory Commission on Public Diplomacy from 1985 to 1998.

MARTIN J. GROSS* is the President of Sandalwood Securities, Inc., a global money management firm. He is also an Adjunct Associate Professor at the Graduate School of International Economics and Finance at Brandeis University and serves on its Board of Overseers.

HENRY GRUNWALD* was Editor in Chief of all of Time, Inc.'s publications from June 1979 to 1987. Mr. Grunwald served as the U.S. Ambassador to Austria from 1988 to 1990, having been appointed by President Ronald Reagan and reappointed by President George H.W. Bush.

BERNARD HAYKEL is an Assistant Professor of Middle Eastern Studies and History at New York University and the author of *Revival and Reform in Islam.*

JOHN W. (JACK) LESLIE JR. is Chairman of Weber Shandwick, the world's leading public relations firm. Formerly a senior aide to Senator Edward M. Kennedy, Mr. Leslie testified before the House

---

*The individual has endorsed the report and submitted an additional or a dissenting view.

International Relations Committee in November 2001 at hearings on U.S. public diplomacy.

BETTE BAO LORD* is Chairman Emeritus of Freedom House, a non-partisan organization dedicated to the promotion of democracy for over 60 years. From 1994 to 2000, she was a Governor of the U.S. Broadcasting Board of Governors, which oversees the Voice of America, Radio Free Europe/Radio Liberty, and Radio Free Asia. Ms. Lord is a best-selling author of fiction and non-fiction books on China.

LEWIS MANILOW* served in the Advisory Commission on Public Diplomacy for ten years, seven years as Chair. He also served as Chairman of the Middle East Subcommittee of the National Democratic Institute for International Affairs.

RANDOLPH MARTIN is the Senior Director for Operations with the International Rescue Committee. Mr. Martin has lived and worked in North Africa and Pakistan for nearly a decade and continues to work closely with IRC programs in these regions and around the world.

SCOTT MILLER is a political and corporate strategist with a wide range of clients worldwide. He is the founder of Core Strategy Group and the former President and founder of the Sawyer/Miller Group.

DAVID E. MOREY is the founder, President, and Chief Executive Officer of DMG, Inc., and a partner in Core Strategy Group, one of the leading strategic communications consultants in America. He is currently Adjunct Professor of International Affairs at Columbia University, specializing in media and politics.

M. ISHAQ NADIRI is the Jay Gould Professor of Economics at New York University's Department of Economics. In addition to his scholarly pursuits, Professor Nadiri is an advisor to Hamid Karzai and the government of Afghanistan.

NANCY NIELSEN is Senior Director of Domestic and International Alliances at Pfizer, Inc. Previously she was Vice President of Corporate Communications at the New York Times Company. During the past decade, she has done pro bono work at the United Nations, the World Bank, and the Carnegie Commission on Preventing Deadly Conflict.

HAROLD PACHIOS is the Chairman of the U.S. Advisory Commission on Public Diplomacy. Mr. Pachios was assistant to Bill Moyers at the Peace Corps in the agency's earliest days and later served in the Johnson administration as Associate White House Press Secretary.

NORMAN J. PATTIZ* is the founder and Chairman of Westwood One, the country's largest radio network company. Mr. Pattiz serves on the U.S. Broadcasting Board of Governors, which oversees all U.S. nonmilitary international broadcasting.

PETER G. PETERSON, Chair of the Independent Task Force on Public Diplomacy, is the Chairman of the Council on Foreign Relations and Chairman and co-founder of the Blackstone Group. Prior to founding Blackstone in 1985, Mr. Peterson served as Chairman and Chief Executive Officer of Lehman Brothers for ten years. He was Secretary of Commerce in the Nixon administration and also served as Assistant to President Richard Nixon on international economic affairs. He is Chairman of the Institute for International Economics and Co-Chairman of the Conference Board Commission on Public Trust and Private Enterprise.

RICHARD L. PLEPLER is the Executive Vice President of Home Box Office, where he has worked for the past eleven years. Prior to that, Mr. Plepler was president of RLP Inc., a production and communications consulting company, which he founded in 1985. Before starting his consultancy, he was a special assistant to Senator Christopher Dodd of Connecticut.

---

*The individual has endorsed the report and submitted an additional or a dissenting view.

MOEEN QURESHI is the Chairman of Emerging Markets Partnership (EMP), a Washington-based asset management company that he co-founded in 1992. He served as Prime Minister of Pakistan for an interim period in 1993 and as Senior Vice President of Operations at the World Bank.

WALTER R. ROBERTS* started his government career with the Voice of America and retired as Associate Director of the U.S. Information Agency, then USIA's top career position. Dr. Roberts was appointed by President George H.W. Bush and reappointed by President Bill Clinton to the U.S. Advisory Commission on Public Diplomacy and serves on the board of the Public Diplomacy Institute of George Washington University.

WILLIAM A. RUGH* was a career U.S. Foreign Service Officer from 1964 to 1995. He served as Ambassador to Yemen and the United Arab Emirates and as U.S. Information Agency Area Director for the Near East, North Africa, and South Asia. Since 1995, Ambassador Rugh has been President and Chief Executive Officer of AMIDEAST. Among his publications is *The Arab Press.*

JILL A. SCHUKER is Senior Vice President and Managing Director for International Operations and Public Affairs at the Kamber Group (TKG), an international strategic communications firm headquartered in Washington, D.C. Prior to joining TKG, she served in the Clinton administration as Special Assistant to the President for National Security Affairs and as Senior Director for Public Affairs at the National Security Council.

JENNIFER SIEG, Director of the Independent Task Force on Public Diplomacy, is Assistant Director of the Outreach Program at the Council on Foreign Relations.

RON SILVER was the founder of the Creative Coalition and its President from 1989 to 1993. Mr. Silver is a member of the Program Committee of the Woodrow Wilson International Center for Scholars and a founding member of the Board of Directors for New York City Public/Private Initiatives, Inc. He was also President of Actor's Equity Association from 1991 to 2000 and Mayor Giuliani's Chairman for the Millennium Committee 1999 to 2001, Office of the Mayor.

ELLIOT STEIN is the Chairman of Caribbean International News Corporation and Director of several private companies. Mr. Stein is a Trustee of Claremont Graduate University, the New School University, and the Annenberg School for Communications at the University of Southern California.

SHIBLEY TELHAMI is the Anwar Sadat Professor for Peace and Development at the University of Maryland and Senior Fellow at the Saban Center at the Brookings Institution. He is the author of a new book, *The Stakes: America and the Middle East.*

JAMES J. ZOGBY is founder and President of the Arab American Institute, a Washington, D.C.–based organization that serves as the political and policy research arm of the Arab American community. He is also the host of a weekly call-in program, "Viewpoint," on Abu Dhabi Television and Worldlink TV. Since 1992, Dr. Zogby has also written a weekly column on U.S. politics for the major newspapers of the Arab world. The column, "Washington Watch," is currently published in fourteen Arab countries. He has authored a number of books including two recent publications, *What Ethnic Americans Really Think* and *What Arabs Think: Values, Beliefs, and Concerns.*

BARRY ZORTHIAN* is a Partner in the Washington, D.C., firm of Alcalde & Fay. From 1996 to 2001, he was President of the Public Diplomacy Council. He is a retired Vice President of Time, Inc., and a retired Foreign Service Officer with thirteen years with the Voice of America and seven years in India and Vietnam, where he was the Chief U.S. Spokesman during the war. From 1990 to 1994, through appointment by President George H.W. Bush, he was a member of the Board for International Broadcasting with oversight of Radio Free Europe/Radio Liberty.

---

*The individual has endorsed the report and submitted an additional or a dissenting view.

APPENDIXES

APPENDIX A

State Department Organizational Reforms

When the U.S. Information Agency was merged into the Department of State in 1999, the president's intent was to put public diplomacy at "the heart of American foreign policy." The personal leadership of the secretary of state and of a few savvy diplomats and the war on terrorism are generating a new enthusiasm for public diplomacy. But four years later, there has been little real change in the State Department's culture or its public diplomacy priorities. Organizational changes alone are not the answer, but the right organizational changes over time can make a positive difference, as the Goldwater-Nichols Act demonstrated in bringing about military reforms. Furthermore, steps should be taken to strengthen the State Department's information and educational exchange programs and to continually upgrade the rank and status of those responsible for public diplomacy across the board. Specifically, the Task Force recommends the following steps:

- Reaffirm that public diplomacy is central to the work of all ambassadors and diplomats, that bold initiatives will be rewarded, risks expected, occasional mistakes accepted, and the absence of requisite skills penalized;

- Provide increased budget and operational authority to the undersecretary of state for public diplomacy and public affairs;

- Make public diplomacy the full-time responsibility of deputy assistant secretaries in the State Department's regional bureaus;

- Initiate and make routine collaborative personnel exchanges between the State Department, other U.S. government departments, and NGOs;

- Require at least one public diplomacy assignment or formal public diplomacy training program for advancement to the senior foreign service;

- Recruit, train, and assign public diplomacy professionals to specialize in countries and regions;

- Recruit private sector experts with public diplomacy skills for non-career appointments abroad;

- Maintain legislated public diplomacy budget protection within the Department of State's diplomatic and consular programs budget, or "150 account"; and

- Clarify and strengthen the secretary of state's role and responsibilities as an ex officio member of the Broadcasting Board of Governors.

State Department Program Reforms:
- Significantly expand the use of the State Department's multi-language Internet websites, streaming audio and video, and leased satellite TV and FM radio broadcasting channels; enhance the State Department's websites with increased marketing and branding;

- Strengthen the Office of International Information Programs through integration of all information operations to include the American Embassy TV Network and Foreign Press Centers. Moreover, substantially increase funding, bureau status, and leadership, raising the status of the director to the level of assistant secretary;

- Give the American Embassy TV Network greater capability to acquire and produce audio and video feeds and Internet streaming for foreign news organizations.

Embassy Operations and Exchanges:
- Significantly expand public diplomacy field staffing and exchanges based on public diplomacy readiness standards and assessments. Readiness criteria should include professional

credentials, language skills, area expertise, flexibility, foreign national staffs, and NGO partnerships.

- Build and improve embassy databases of influential people and stakeholders. Train embassy officers in developing attitudinal segmented categories and in targeting strategies and priorities along a continuum of support for U.S. foreign policies, including "hard support," "soft support," and "undecided." In fact, new attitudinal research and target marketing techniques show it is six times more expensive and difficult to move "undecided" consumers to the category of "soft support" than it is to move "soft support" to "hard support." This suggests that attitudinal research, conducted properly, is an important tool for prioritizing future public diplomacy efforts and increasing their effectiveness and efficiency.

- Mandate comprehensive exchange alumni databases and use of the Internet to network and advance communities of interest among exchange alumni.

Building Cross-Cultural Initiatives:
- Develop cross-cultural initiatives for countries with large Muslim populations with new funding of up to $1 billion annually—targeted at students, scholars, and media. This will permit expansion of traditional programs such as Fulbright exchanges and allow the reopening of public libraries where Internet penetration is low. In addition, selectively offer cable or satellite television programming and initiate new activities such as a U.S.-based press institute that could train Islamic journalists and publish objective critiques of the Islamic press.

APPENDIX B

DRAFT MISSION PROGRAM PLAN ON PUBLIC DIPLOMACY

This generic draft Mission Program Plan (MPP) statement on public diplomacy should flow from the proposal for a presidential directive and for a Public Diplomacy Coordinating Structure. It is intended to fulfill a foreign post's commitment to carrying out the secretary of state's mandate to significantly increase public diplomacy initiatives.

Chief of Mission Duties:
The secretary of state directs the chief of mission (COM) to take whatever steps are necessary and appropriate, consistent with directives from the Department of State, to redeploy mission assets (personnel, budget, etc.) in order to prepare a new public diplomacy initiative. The COM shall now be responsible for directly supervising and directing all elements of a foreign post's public diplomacy programs including:

- Press attaché activities;

- Public appearances by all foreign post personnel;

- Representation expenditures by the COM, the deputy chief of mission (DCM), and the political, economic and press sections;

- Visits by military personnel and assets, including all humanitarian programs;

- Cultural programs;

- Fulbright Scholarship, International Visitor, and other exchange programs; and

- Assistance programs administered by other agencies (USAID, the Departments of Commerce, Agriculture, and Defense, etc.)

that may directly or indirectly have a favorable impact on the U.S. image in the host country.

Public Diplomacy Objectives:
In the wake of September 11 and the escalation of violence in the Middle East, the United States faces daunting challenges to improve receptivity to its foreign policy objectives and to open channels of communications with opinion leaders who are adverse to U.S. policies. Within the current budget constraints, the COM plans to redirect foreign post resources to achieving the following objectives:

1. Complete an assessment of the key policy and message elements that need to be promoted to local constituencies;

2. Determine ways to measure impact and capacity to recalibrate methods and targets as needed;

3. Identify and prioritize key public opinion targets;

4. Assess how best to mobilize foreign post resources to accomplish key objectives;

5. Determine how to provide regular feedback to the Department of State to help determine the effectiveness of each foreign post's programs against other MPP public diplomacy programs in the Middle East and in other parts of the world.

The Department of State believes that one of the highest priorities a foreign post faces is to develop creatively new public diplomacy opportunities and programs within its current budgetary authority.

Mission Plans:

1. The COM plans to coordinate and organize an initiative in all foreign posts to identify potential speaking opportunities before the following organizations:

   • Boards of editors of local newspapers;

- Reporters;

- Civil society organizations;

- University student organizations and faculty organizations;

- Television and radio stations;

- Theological seminaries;

- Political party organizations;

- Scientific and technical organizations;

- Military and diplomatic educational institutions.

2. Each foreign post will establish a Public Diplomacy Task Force, chaired by the DCM that shall meet no less than weekly to coordinate all public diplomacy activities. The Public Diplomacy Task Force will include the attachés (no substitutes) of each mission element assigned to the foreign post. The foreign post will establish a coordinating committee of NGOs represented in the country, which will meet monthly with mission elements. The foreign post will maintain listservs and other web-based links to the NGO community.

3. The foreign post will assess the language abilities of key personnel. All attachés will be required to undertake a State Department–organized instruction course on public diplomacy and media presentation.

4. The foreign post will plan to negotiate media placements for weekly op-ed pieces of the COM with key media elements in the country.

5. The COM will host a bi-weekly "reporter's roundtable," inviting reporters to the residence to have both on-the-record and off-the-record conversations with the ambassador.

6. The foreign post will identify key American public figures, including internationally recognized cultural and media icons, who may be invited to the foreign post to participate in policy

debates. The foreign post will assess the local private sector's ability to sponsor such visits in view of budgetary limitations.

7. The foreign post will take an inventory of information available to the media in local languages and advise the Department of State of any gaps that the foreign post believes need to be filled in order to open consistent blast fax and other distribution capabilities with local media outlets.

8. Working with the local American Chamber of Commerce and representatives of the private sector, the COM will develop plans for no fewer than two delegations of key opinion leaders to visit the United States during the coming calendar year.

9. The DCM will assume responsibility, as chair of the Public Diplomacy Task Force, of shifting resources as needed to fulfill these objectives.

10. The foreign post plans to work with U.S. technology companies to develop in-country "e-government" initiatives to help plan for Internet information exchanges between local educational institutions and sources of information about the United States. The foreign post will also translate the official embassy website into the local language and saturate local media and Internet service providers with the foreign post's website address to attract "hits" to the site's information about America.

11. All surplus foreign post funds shall be transferred to a multi-year public diplomacy account, to be directly administered by the COM. These funds shall be used to supplement ongoing public diplomacy initiatives that otherwise cannot be achieved due to other budgetary constraints.

12. The foreign post reporting will reflect increased outreach to key contacts by all mission elements and will provide sustained in-depth analysis of influence structures and the information environment in the country.

13. The COM will provide the Department of State with a public diplomacy roadmap in the Mission Program Plan, updated as circumstances warrant, analyzing publics, communications channels, and U.S. policy objectives in the country. Key questions to be answered include: Who is influential? What media do they use? How important is it to U.S. interests that the mission communicates with them? In addition, the COM will identify clear priorities and tradeoffs among the major instruments of public diplomacy, including exchanges, international broadcasting, partnership projects with NGOs, as well as mission information and cultural programs. The COM's analysis will be a central element in the Quadrennial Public Diplomacy Review.

APPENDIX C

U.S. International Broadcasting

The United States established the Voice of America (VOA) in 1942. Radio Free Europe and Radio Liberty (RFE/RL), U.S.-funded stations separate from VOA, originated in the early 1950s. They acted as "surrogate" national radios for listeners in Eastern Europe and the Soviet Union who were denied free media in their own countries. Surrogate broadcasting services to Cuba, Asia, Iraq, and Iran were established in the 1980s and 1990s; RFE/RL initiated Radio Free Afghanistan in 2002. Moreover, the International Broadcasting Act of 1994 consolidated all nonmilitary U.S. international broadcasting under a part-time bipartisan Broadcasting Board of Governors (BBG). The president, with the advice and consent of the Senate, appoints eight BBG members, and the secretary of state serves on the board ex officio "to provide information and guidance on foreign policy issues." The BBG is authorized "to direct and supervise" all civilian broadcasting activities of the U.S. government.

These broadcasting services comprise about half of the government's nonmilitary public diplomacy budget. The president's fiscal year 2003 request for the U.S. international broadcasting budget totals $518 million. (The combined fiscal year 2003 request for the State Department's information and educational exchange programs is $540 million.) These broadcasting services have brand identities and are staffed with dedicated journalism professionals. Moreover, the BBG and many of its supporters in Congress believe the BBG has a responsibility to serve as a "firewall" that separates U.S. international broadcasters and the foreign policy community, ensuring journalistic objectivity and credibility.[10]

Today, the United States broadcasts in more than 60 languages. In some countries, U.S. broadcasters have sizeable market shares; in others, particularly in the Middle East, audiences are typically small. Listening rates can be high in a crisis and in regions where credible alternative news sources are limited. In competitive media environments, however, audiences for U.S. broadcasting are much smaller, and program and research costs rise dramatically.

Washington has recently undertaken several promising initiatives to deal with today's crowded media marketplace. For example, just months after September 11, the BBG launched youth-oriented Radio Sawa throughout the Middle East. Budgeted at over $30 million, Sawa targets radio programming to a "new young mainstream" of educated Arabs under 30 and an "emerging Arab leadership." The station broadcasts a mix of popular music, features, news, roundtables, call-in shows, and talk programming. Sawa's focus and audience segmentation reflect a significant change in U.S. international broadcasting priorities. Radio Sawa has quickly built a substantial audience throughout the region and inspired the administration to fund a proposed Middle East Television Network (METN). In February 2002, the BBG also began broadcasting Radio Farda, a youth-oriented Persian-language effort throughout Iran.

If audience research and analysis shows it to be successful, the Task Force supports additional efforts to: (1) replicate these media efforts in customized ways around the world; (2) recruit, train, and involve young, capable, and creative journalists and commentators; (3) further explore ways to adapt and apply this approach to tele-

---

[10]U.S. international broadcasting serves America's interests by providing audiences "comprehensive, accurate and objective news information," by "representing American society and culture," and by "presenting the policies of the United States." See Voice of America Charter, Public Law 94-350 and Broadcasting Board of Governors, 1999–2000 Annual Report, p. 2, www.ibb.gov/bbg/report.html. "A separate governing board to supervise the broadcasting entities—the Broadcasting Board of Governors—is essential to providing what I call an 'asbestos firewall,' that is, an arms-length distance between the broadcasters and the foreign policy bureaucracy that assures journalistic integrity and independence." Statement of Senator Joseph R. Biden Jr., March 6, 1997.

vision; (4) enhance continually the marketing and operating of these projects; and (5) receive additional resources and funding.

In the near future, U.S. international broadcasting faces four major challenges:

- *Emerging technologies*
As discussed in the report, the Internet, digital radio, direct satellite broadcasting, and other technologies are changing the global media environment. Successfully managing the transition from short-wave to alternative technologies is one key issue. Another is whether U.S. broadcasters will move successfully into the world of interactive and highly personalized technologies that allow programming on demand, that separate communications channels and media content, and that emphasize narrowcasting rather than broadcasting.

- *Television*
The medium of choice in many countries, including those in the Middle East, is television. While the administration has shown a commitment in this area by funding and supporting a new Middle Eastern satellite television initiative,[11] the vast majority of U.S. international broadcasting resources is devoted to short-wave and AM/FM radio. Sunken costs, insufficient funding, and institutional traditions tied to radio and short-wave have prevented U.S. broadcasters from using TV to reach new audiences in key markets. Certainly, radio is still important in many countries. But how, whether, and when to use television through the U.S. international broadcasting services, the Department of State, and commercial media are key questions for policymakers and for Congress.

- *Language service and program priorities*
The International Broadcasting Act requires the BBG to conduct annual reviews to determine "the addition and deletion"

---

[11]President Bush initially requested $30 million for the creation of a U.S-sponsored satellite television network to be broadcast in Arabic. In the emergency supplemental appropriations bill for fiscal 2003, Congress approved an additional $32 million to get the project on the air before the end of the year.

of language services. Issues to be addressed include: How much should the United States invest in languages where audiences are small, as a hedge against future needs? How should surge capacities be developed and maintained? How should programs be improved so they have relevance and immediacy in countries important to U.S. interests? To what extent should the United States broadcast in Albanian and Serbian in Kosovo? Does the United States need an RFE/RL service in Afghanistan in addition to its Voice of America services? Should RFE/RL broadcast in the Avar, Chechen, and Circassian languages in the North Caucasus? Is Cuban-directed TV Marti cost-effective?

These are important questions not just for broadcasters, but also for policymakers and for the development of a sound public diplomacy strategy. To be sure, decisions on broadcast languages ultimately are political decisions. Too often policymakers and legislators leave the hard questions on broadcasting priorities to the BBG and usually become engaged only as a consequence of ad hoc diplomatic or political pressures. But the national interest will be served by a considered and sustained involvement in strategic broadcasting issues by the National Security Council, the State Department, and America's elected political leaders.

- *Broadcasting's role in national security*
  Credibility, journalistic integrity, program quality, and accurate news are important. Important, too, are decisions on funding priorities, language priorities, and how to define relations between the BBG, the Department of State, and the National Security Council. Moreover, the president, the Department of State, and Congress must all give higher priority to dealing with these long-standing issues as part of any successful public diplomacy strategy. And, again, while preserving the independence intended in the International Broadcasting Act of 1994, all U.S. international broadcasting activities should be strategically coordinated and overseen by the proposed Public Diplomacy Coordinating Structure.

U.S. international broadcasting has long stood at the crossroads of journalism and foreign policy. Everyone agrees that broadcasts should be truthful and that high program quality is increasingly necessary to attract listeners and viewers in information-rich media environments. But the management of international broadcasting and decisions on language priorities raise more difficult questions.

Over the next decade, for example, should a part-time BBG continue to direct and to supervise U.S. broadcasting services? What does it mean operationally for the secretary of state to provide "information and guidance on foreign policy issues," as required by the International Broadcasting Act of 1994? What is the appropriate role of the National Security Council in international broadcasting decisions? Are decisions on language services so vitally linked to "national security" that they should be made by the executive branch and by Congress? Or do they have more to do with "broadcasting," and should the BBG, as required by the act, continue to make these decisions using "such criteria as audience size and awareness of the broadcasts in target areas, media environment, political and economic freedom, programming quality, transmission effectiveness, cost, broadcast hours, and language overlap between broadcasters."[12]

The Task Force believes these are important long-term questions that deserve increased attention from the Department of State, the National Security Council, Congress, and the BBG. Many, of course, fall within the purview of the new Public Diplomacy Coordinating Structure recommended in the report. Moreover, as a priority, a General Accounting Office study of the effectiveness of the management structure created by the International Broadcasting Act of 1994 will be of assistance in addressing these issues. In addition, the proposed Independent Public Diplomacy Training Institute (IPDI) should add experience and creativity to America's international broadcasting efforts.

Finally, the Task Force supports an independent and well-qualified broadcasting board with a full-time, top-caliber chief exec-

---

[12]U.S. International Broadcasting Act, Public Law 103-236.

utive officer who would report to the current BBG and be empow-
ered to direct and supervise all U.S. nonmilitary international broadcasting activities. Furthermore, the Department of State and the
BBG should strengthen the secretary of state's role in
providing information and guidance on foreign policy to the
BBG by clarifying and specifying the secretary's role in making
decisions on broadcast languages and other foreign policy matters.

APPENDIX D

ADDITIONAL DATA ON WORLD OPINION

The following charts are provided courtesy of the Pew Research Center for the People & the Press. They appear here in a slightly altered version from the Pew Global Attitudes Project's "Views of a Changing World, June 2003."

Dislike of the U.S. Spreads and Deepens in the Muslim World

--- *Favorable Opinion of U.S.* ---

	1999/ 2000 %	Summer 2002 %	Today %
Kuwait	–	–	63
Nigeria*	–	72	38
Lebanon*	–	30	15
Turkey	52	30	15
Indonesia	75	61	15
Pakistan	23	10	12
Jordan	–	25	1
Palestinian Auth.	–	–	1
Israeli Arabs	–	–	36
Israeli Jews	–	–	86

* Based on Muslims only.

U.S. Ratings Still Markedly Lower Than in 2002

--- *Favorable Opinion of U.S.* ---

	1999/ 2000 %	Summer 2002 %	Today %
Great Britain	83	75	70
Canada	71	72	63
Italy	76	70	60
South Korea	58	53	46
Germany	78	61	45
France	62	63	43
Russia	37	61	36
Brazil	56	52	35

More See Threats to Islam

See serious threats to Islam today ...

	2002 %	2003 %
Jordan	81	97
Lebanon	74	73
Pakistan	28	64
Indonesia	33	59
Turkey	35	50
Nigeria	21	42
Palestinian Authority	–	91
Kuwait	–	63

Question asked of Muslim respondents only. Trends shown where available. Question not permitted in Egypt.

Worried About Potential U.S. Military Threat

Not Worried	Worried

Country	Not Worried	Worried
Indonesia	26%	74%
Nigeria	27%	72%
Pakistan	23%	72%
Russia	26%	71%
Turkey	27%	71%
Lebanon	41%	58%
Jordan	44%	56%
Kuwait	44%	53%
Morocco	52%	46%

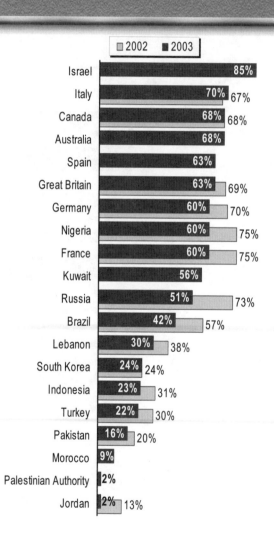

Support U.S.-Led War on Terrorism

Modest Confidence in Bush Worldwide

	First	Second	Third
U.S.	Blair (83%)	**Bush (78%)**	Sharon (49%)
Canada	Blair (75%)	**Bush (59%)**	Putin (54%)
G. Britain	Annan (72%)	Blair (71%)	Putin (53%)
France	Schroeder (76%)	Chirac (75%)	Annan (65%)
Germany	Chirac (84%)	Putin (75%)	Annan (74%)
Italy	Annan (69%)	Blair (57%)	Chirac (46%)
Spain	Annan (59%)	Chirac (51%)	Schroeder (48%)
Brazil	Annan (32%)	Chirac (31%)	Schroeder (22%)
Australia	Blair (80%)	Annan (68%)	**Bush (59%)**
S. Korea	Annan (47%)	Chirac (47%)	Blair (41%)
Russia	Putin (76%)	Chirac (42%)	Schroeder (40%)
Israel	**Bush (83%)**	Blair (76%)	Sharon (68%)

Percent saying they have "a lot" or "some" confidence in each leader's ability to do the right thing regarding world affairs.

[87]

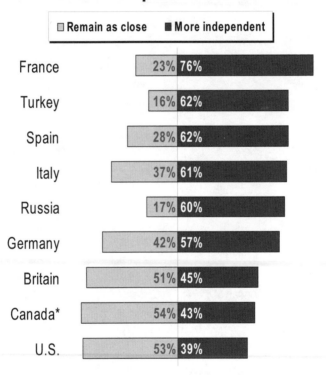

Most Europeans Want a Less Close Partnership

U.S.-European Alliance

☐ Remain as close ■ More independent

	Remain as close	More independent
France	23%	76%
Turkey	16%	62%
Spain	28%	62%
Italy	37%	61%
Russia	17%	60%
Germany	42%	57%
Britain	51%	45%
Canada*	54%	43%
U.S.	53%	39%

* Canadians asked about relationship between Canada and the U.S.

Allied Effort to Avoid Civilian Casualties

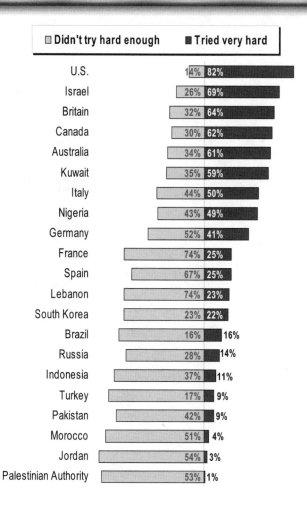

	☐ Didn't try hard enough	■ Tried very hard
U.S.	14%	82%
Israel	26%	69%
Britain	32%	64%
Canada	30%	62%
Australia	34%	61%
Kuwait	35%	59%
Italy	44%	50%
Nigeria	43%	49%
Germany	52%	41%
France	74%	25%
Spain	67%	25%
Lebanon	74%	23%
South Korea	23%	22%
Brazil	16%	16%
Russia	28%	14%
Indonesia	37%	11%
Turkey	17%	9%
Pakistan	42%	9%
Morocco	51%	4%
Jordan	54%	3%
Palestinian Authority	53%	1%

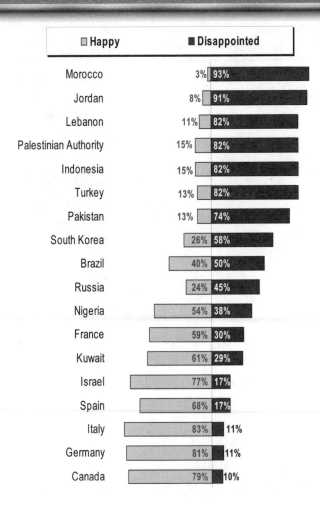

Reaction to Lack of Iraqi Military Resistance

	□ Happy	■ Disappointed
Morocco	3%	93%
Jordan	8%	91%
Lebanon	11%	82%
Palestinian Authority	15%	82%
Indonesia	15%	82%
Turkey	13%	82%
Pakistan	13%	74%
South Korea	26%	58%
Brazil	40%	50%
Russia	24%	45%
Nigeria	54%	38%
France	59%	30%
Kuwait	61%	29%
Israel	77%	17%
Spain	68%	17%
Italy	83%	11%
Germany	81%	11%
Canada	79%	10%

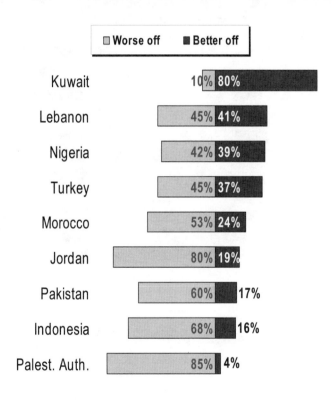

Postwar Iraq
Without Saddam,
Iraqi people will be ...

	☐ Worse off	■ Better off
Kuwait	10%	80%
Lebanon	45%	41%
Nigeria	42%	39%
Turkey	45%	37%
Morocco	53%	24%
Jordan	80%	19%
Pakistan	60%	17%
Indonesia	68%	16%
Palest. Auth.	85%	4%

Postwar Iraq
Allied job addressing needs of Iraqi people

	☐ Fair/Poor	■ Excellent/Good

Country	Fair/Poor	Excellent/Good
U.S.	32%	59%
Nigeria	34%	59%
Kuwait	40%	53%
France	54%	45%
Britain	50%	41%
Canada	46%	41%
Australia	53%	40%
Italy	52%	36%
Brazil	54%	31%
Israel	60%	29%
Spain	64%	26%
Lebanon	70%	25%
Germany	70%	23%
Turkey	63%	23%
Jordan	80%	14%
Pakistan	60%	13%
Indonesia	83%	12%
Morocco	67%	11%
South Korea	84%	10%
Russia	78%	10%
Palestinian Authority	87%	7%

Western-Style Democracy "Can Work Here"

	2002 %	2003 %
Nigeria	76	75
Lebanon	69	68
Jordan	63	68
Pakistan	45	58
Turkey	43	50
Indonesia	64	41
Kuwait	–	83
Morocco	–	64
Senegal	87	–
Ghana	83	–
Uzbekistan	83	–
Ivory Coast	82	–
Uganda	77	–
Mali	76	–
Tanzania	64	–
Bangladesh	57	–

Based on Muslim populations.

SELECTED REPORTS OF INDEPENDENT TASK FORCES
SPONSORED BY THE COUNCIL ON FOREIGN RELATIONS

* †*Emergency Responders: Drastically Underfunded, Dangerously Unprepared* (2003)
  Warren B. Rudman, Chair; Richard A. Clarke, Senior Adviser; Jamie F. Metzl,
  Project Director
* †*Meeting the North Korean Nuclear Challenge* (2003)
  Morton I. Abramowitz and James T. Laney, Co-Chairs; Eric Heginbotham,
  Project Director
* †*Burma: Time for Change* (2003)
  Mathea Falco, Chair
* †*Chinese Military Power* (2003)
  Harold Brown, Chair; Joseph W. Prueher, Vice Chair; Adam Segal,
  Project Director
* †*Iraq: The Day After* (2003)
  Thomas R. Pickering and James R. Schlesinger, Co-Chairs; Eric P.
  Schwartz, Project Director
* †*Threats to Democracy* (2002)
  Madeleine K. Albright and Bronislaw Geremek, Co-Chairs; Morton H.
  Halperin, Project Director; Elizabeth Frawley Bagley, Associate Director
* †*America—Still Unprepared, Still in Danger* (2002)
  Gary Hart and Warren B. Rudman, Co-Chairs; Stephen Flynn, Project Director
* †*Terrorist Financing* (2002)
  Maurice R. Greenberg, Chair; William F. Wechsler and Lee S. Wolosky, Project
  Co-Directors
* †*Enhancing U.S. Leadership at the United Nations* (2002)
  David Dreier and Lee H. Hamilton, Co-Chairs; Lee Feinstein and Adrian Karat-
  nycky, Project Co-Directors
* †*Testing North Korea: The Next Stage in U.S. and ROK Policy* (2001)
  Morton I. Abramowitz and James T. Laney, Co-Chairs; Robert A. Manning,
  Project Director
* †*The United States and Southeast Asia: A Policy Agenda for the New Administration*
  (2001)
  J. Robert Kerrey, Chair; Robert A. Manning, Project Director
* †*Strategic Energy Policy: Challenges for the 21st Century* (2001)
  Edward L. Morse, Chair; Amy Myers Jaffe, Project Director
* †*State Department Reform* (2001)
  Frank C. Carlucci, Chair; Ian J. Brzezinski, Project Coordinator;
  Cosponsored with the Center for Strategic and International Studies
* †*U.S.-Cuban Relations in the 21st Century: A Follow-on Report* (2001)
  Bernard W. Aronson and William D. Rogers, Co-Chairs; Julia Sweig and Walter
  Mead, Project Directors
* †*A Letter to the President and a Memorandum on U.S. Policy Toward Brazil* (2001)
  Stephen Robert, Chair; Kenneth Maxwell, Project Director
* †*Toward Greater Peace and Security in Colombia* (2000)
  Bob Graham and Brent Scowcroft, Co-Chairs; Michael Shifter, Project Director;
  Cosponsored with the Inter-American Dialogue
  †*Future Directions for U.S. Economic Policy Toward Japan* (2000)
  Laura D'Andrea Tyson, Chair; M. Diana Helweg Newton, Project Director
* †*Promoting Sustainable Economies in the Balkans* (2000)
  Steven Rattner, Chair; Michael B. G. Froman, Project Director
* †*Nonlethal Technologies: Progress and Prospects* (1999)
  Richard L. Garwin, Chair; W. Montague Winfield, Project Director
* †*U.S. Policy Toward North Korea: Next Steps* (1999)
  Morton I. Abramowitz and James T. Laney, Co-Chairs; Michael J. Green, Project
  Director

†Available on the Council on Foreign Relations website at www.cfr.org.
*Available from Brookings Institution Press. To order, call 800-275-1447.